Navigating the Postmodern Condition

Drawing on poststructuralist frameworks, this book examines the way to a radical acceptance of daily discontinuities and difference as it allows us to embrace life in the postmodern world.

With each chapter exploring the human relationship with a disjunction in daily life, such as sleeping, forgetting, and multitasking, the author examines overlooked aspects of daily living as fresh data from which to analyze our condition. A phenomenological study of postmodern life, the book provides anecdotes of what it is like to live through these gaps and theorizes how we use these gaps. Using an arts-based methodology, the author also allows the work to mirror the discontinuities which it describes, interrupting the assumption of our lives as continuous and unitary in both form and content. Addressing the vast jumble of contradictions that is our daily experience in this contemporary world, it offers explanation through theory and anecdote and illustrates the path toward radical acceptance, which allows us to see ourselves as beautifully composed of fractures, gaps, and overflow.

It will appeal to scholars, researchers, and postgraduate students with interests in poststructuralism, curriculum theory, and art-based research methods.

Wade A. Tillett is Professor at the University of Wisconsin – Whitewater, USA.

Navigating the Postmodern Condition

The Discontinuities of Everyday Life

Wade A. Tillett

NEW YORK AND LONDON

First published 2024
by Routledge
605 Third Avenue, New York, NY 10158

and by Routledge
4 Park Square, Milton Park, Abingdon, Oxon, OX14 4RN

Routledge is an imprint of the Taylor & Francis Group, an informa business

ISBN: 978-1-032-71561-2 (hbk)
ISBN: 978-1-032-74995-2 (pbk)
ISBN: 978-1-003-47188-2 (ebk)

DOI: 10.4324/ 9781003471882

Typeset in Times New Roman
by Apex CoVantage, LLC

Contents

Preface

~

What is lost moment by moment is more than what is preserved. How can we show this balance, this precarity? Not just with examples from daily life but through the enactment of those chasms? That is, how can writing (or art, or doing) foreground the negative space?

I don't want this to be a description of gaps. I want it to make us feel them more, use them more, value them more. I want to shift our perception to the spaces between.

I want to inhabit the absence for a while, be still within it, see what comes. I'm not sure how to do that.

I wanted to tell you, I wanted to tell myself, that it is OK to be hypocritical, disjointed, and flawed. We can never be fully aware no matter how much meditating we do. Being overwhelmed and displaced are basic to life itself. We rely on and use those things to our advantage – consciously and unconsciously. I don't want to just say it, because I just did and I am unsatisfied; I want to feel it, to use it as new media with which to partly craft these lives. Here are some tools you are using you didn't even know you had! Aha! I wish you would say. I wish I would say.

~

I think of this project as having users rather than readers.[1] I want to draw attention to the way in which users *already* use gaps – and how. It is my hope that a reconceptualization of daily life that includes gaps will allow us to see that we move more freely than we think, that hypocrisies can be escape routes, that the unrecoverable and nonproductive is still part of life – it still counts, that life itself is much messier and more disjointed than the simple descriptions we often operate with. We are not singular. We've never been singular. Look at how we know that and use it, even if only subconsciously sometimes, to our attempted advantage. This may seem a postmodern take on the world, but the nonsingularity of living experience predates not only our time but our species.

~

I am done hedging. Yes, my directions are tentative, but I intend to pursue them with full force. They will not align. I will run in different ways toward conflicting objectives. I will choose tools for each task. I will develop these tools, hone them, share them. I will live a thousand modes. I already live a thousand modes. I will notice them, push them, release them.

~

I am not going to apologize for the contradictions. They are the means by which I escape.

~

Writing is a series of contradictions, of nonconductors, of connections not made. Rather than a grand unified theory, we have microtheories, insulated from one another, deployed or ready to be deployed. Something exists between the writing. Something lives where the writing points to but does not go. Something happens after it leaves off. Abandonments, resistances, contradictions. A multitude of voices and modes. A cacophony. And this is only the cacophony of the written, a small subset of the cacophony of living lives.

But of course, conductors are also employed. Connections and translations are made. While these texts tear themselves in different directions, in some form, they go together. The hope is that we can foreground the nonconductors, as the conductors are well known. Both are needed, of course, but at least in my own life, I find I have too often deployed nonconductors only unconsciously. Here, I attempt to open my eyes to the times I shut them.

~

We are complex stews of purposes – aspirational, inherited, practical.

~

Basic to writing is a "we" that (attempts to) overcome the gaps between us, between author and reader. There is an imposition to this "we," to the assumption that there is something common between us.[2] This is the arrogance and audacity of all writing, of all language. The author imagines that there is a point at which the reader overlaps and can understand, or at least use, the words written. The imposing we is at the heart of writing. It is presupposed. Regardless of point of view, the essential author–imagined reader assumes a commonality, a we.

I want to share a world. I want you to see the same things I see. I want you to touch the same things I touch. I want to communicate.

As a reader, this imposition is felt. We rebel by using the text in different ways, on different planes. We undermine the assumptions. We place the book as a doorstop. We rip out pages to start a fire. We collage.[3] We analyze. We question. And yet.

Something transfers through. Be it only the physicality of the page. Engagement implies a we. Even refusal, ignorance implies a we. The national organization requires that each member receive the organization's journal in their mailbox. There is a "readership" whether or not there are readers. We can take great joy in throwing these journals in to the trash. And yet.

Something falls through. Something does not connect. There is an emptiness to this we. There is a chasm between us, between author and reader.

~

We can't even agree on what is a gap, on what is real. Instead of considering the gap as already real, we ask how does the gap become real? What interests are served? Can we occupy gaps in different ways?[4]

How does naming the "gap" produce the gap?[5] How does it destroy the gap?

And vice versa.[6]

The reality of the gap is also the effect of power. In some cases, it is not real – it was only a dream. In other cases, it is real – death as final and death as the gateway to something even more real, a higher reality.[7]

~

Any space, any punctuation, any carriage return can be the site of an unknown amount of loss.[8] Each space potentially covers a chasm. Each space may conceal an editor's cut, the invisible destruction of days or weeks of work. We read along, leaping over we know not what. The universe is filled with infinite holes, tiny bubbles each containing a universe.[9]

Words themselves conceal. Words throw the reader off the track, provide an alternate, defend, cover the chasm of what is not said, patched over.

Only so much can be said with words anyway. Only so much time can be taken to write things down. Only so much "honesty" can be tolerated.

We inhabit so many disjunctions, so many discontinuities, so easily skipped over. Until they are not, that is. And then we have no choice but to see this world as innumerable worlds, as a cacophony of disjunctions, "as a pure many."[10]

~

The problem is that all my attempts to show randomness end with an overly unifying structure – won't it be the same with gaps? I have tried and failed repeatedly to create structures that allow randomness and choice and participation. Inevitably, the structure is itself overbearing. It is an enabling limit, a grid, a skeleton. A singular experience/work carved/assembled from supposedly disparate pieces. Montage creates a continuity out of discontinuities. Can writing, a tool of production, be used to show the gaps of production?[11] Would that be the useless production of useless things to show they are useless?

~

To look at the structure of gaps is to potentially lose the gaping abyss quality, to demystify, to enclose that which is not to be enclosed,[12] to name the unnamed.[13]

Writing about gaps is not as contradictory as it would first seem. Writing is already always filled with gaps, searching the gaps, riding the gaps. The spaces between letters, words, sentences, paragraphs are already always the potential launching point of a new direction or the covering of an escapade – an edit.

~

To see the gaps is to see the excesses, the abysses, which are our everyday experiences and nonexperiences. To see what is invisible requires more than opening one's eyes. It requires practice in seeing.

Some gaps will remain unknown. Some things remain beyond experience or the knowable. Mysteries will always remain.

~

No matter how we try or try not to capture the gaps in everyday life, "something always escapes."[14] This escaping something is the topic of this book. And yet it must remain beyond and between these words. In many ways, then, the book is doomed from the start. In other ways, perhaps we can create fertile cracks wherein the reader can enact their own slippages and escapes.

In all texts, gaps exist. In this text, we make explicit discussion of how we might use them. But the real work falls between, in the actual use by the user of this text, of these gaps.

A sentence contradicts the one before. A chapter contradicts the one before. This is an opening, a movement, a space.

~

"The writer is a sorcerer."[15] Writing, reading, living are ways of becoming an other. We typically think of reading and writing as squarely within the zone of conscious rationality. The topic here is exactly what escapes, exceeds, and complicates that zone. Upon closer inspection, of course, reading and writing are composed of multiple forces, modes, zones. There are overlaps, juxtapositions, contradictions, leaps, and dead ends. There is emotion, recollection, reworking, wandering. Writing and reading are an open-ended search. It is in this nonclosed mode that the mode can exceed itself. The sorcerer calls upon forces beyond that of the call. Words do things.[16] Words direct things, point to things, align with things. We bend things to our will. Things bend us to their will. We channel forces. Forces channel us. Co-manifestation.[17] We incite something that goes beyond the limits we used to start it with.[18] Something catches fire.

~

Here, then, we write. We conjure. We practice this sorcery. We call forth to the forces. Beyond. Through.

Deep down, we desire: Respond through us. I am your willing vessel.

Lightning rods. Wands. Hoses. Tubes. Wormholes. Blood pulses through.

The purpose of text is always to call forth, to conjure, to enact. Between these incantations, beneath them, is desire.

These texts are to a spellbook what a found object is to art. Look at the spells we already use. How can we use them still? How can we use them differently? How can we abandon the borders of who we are? How can we dis-integrate? How can we join forces as spirits, with spirits? How can I explain to you how easy this is?[19] How much we already do it every day?

Words are part of this. Words are not all of this. They call forth.[20]

Here. Dis-integrate. Abandon. Dis-articulate. Non-conduct. Dis-member.

~

Notes

1 "Accordingly, empiricists are not concerned with determining the essence and intrinsic relation of each thing within a single all-encompassing totality, but with describing how new relations can be actively created between things relative to a specific context in order to produce change in and between the complex unities these relationships form. . . . The processes of creating new relations or altering previously established ones and the effects produced by these transformations assume primacy for radical empiricism. Relations are to be evaluated by their consequences in experience, not by their conformity to an original essence." Hayden, *Multiplicity and Becoming*, 92.

2 "Violence of this *communal* dissymmetry . . . the origin of the *common*, happening each time . . . we call them while *supposing*, that is to say while *imposing* a 'we.'" Derrida, *Archive Fever*, 41.

3 Tillett et al., "A Readers' Rebellion."

4 "To call a presupposition into question is not the same as doing away with it; rather, it is to free it from its metaphysical lodgings in order to understand what political interests were secured in and by that metaphysical placing, and thereby to permit the term to occupy and to serve very different political aims." Butler, *Bodies That Matter*, 30.

5 "[P]erformativity must be understood not as a singular or deliberate 'act,' but rather, as the reiterative and citational practice by which discourse produces the effects that it names." Butler, *Bodies That Matter*, 2.

6 "[B]ut materiality will be rethought as the effect of power, as power's most productive effect." Butler, *Bodies That Matter*, 2.

7 Tillett, "Creating the Real."

8 Derrida put in 52 spaces to mark an unknown amount of text lost, time lost. Derrida, *The Post Card*.

9 Minsky, "Universe Bubbles."

10 James, *Pragmatism*, 68.

11 "The master's tools will never dismantle the master's house." Lorde, *Sister Outsider*. "To pursue the impossible is to fail. But perhaps the dynamics of failure and invention . . . can still be pursued without dishonouring the alterity of the impossible." Koczy, *Beckett, Deleuze and Performance*, 69. "The very act of trying to think the unthinkable will, in Deleuze's account, always risk translating its alterity in to terms we can all-too-easily think and comprehend . . . . we will always run the risk of turning a . . . nothing into something it is not." Koczy, *Beckett, Deleuze and Performance*, 83. "We should not assume that the epistemic tools we have

developed for the study of knowledge or the theories we have developed concerning knowledge practices will transfer to the study of ignorance." Tuana, "Coming to Understand," 226.

12 "To have the concept of matter is to lose the exteriority that the concept is supposed to secure." Butler, *Bodies That Matter*, 31.

13 "[I]gnorance (is) that which is beyond the grasp of knowledge but can be gestured toward by examining the performative aspects of knowledge production." Malewski and Jaramillo, *Ignorance*, 11.

14 "Everything you can think of, however vast or inclusive, has on the pluralistic view a genuinely 'external' environment of some sort or amount. Things are 'with' one another in many ways, but nothing includes everything, or dominates over everything. The word 'and' trails along after every sentence. Something always escapes. 'Ever not quite' has to be said of the best attempts made anywhere in the universe at attaining all-inclusiveness. . . . However much may be collected, however much may report itself as present at any effective center of consciousness or action, something else is self-governed and absent and unreduced to unity." James, *A Pluralistic Universe*, 274.

15 "If the writer is a sorcerer, it is because writing is a becoming, writing is traversed by strange becomings that are not becomings-writer, but becomings-rat, becomings-insect, becomings-wolf, etc." Deleuze and Guattari, *A Thousand Plateaus*, 240. "Sometimes I put the imagination to a more rare use. I choose words, images, and body sensations and animate them to impress them on my consciousness, thereby making changes in my belief system and reprogramming my consciousness." Anzaldua, *Borderlands / La Frontera*, 70. "I write the myths in me, the myths I am, the myths I want to become." Anzaldua, *Borderlands /La Frontera*, 71.

16 "[Research] is, instead, a form of action itself – an ontological intervention or a series of varied interventions in the service of the necessarily mutable project." Rosiek and Kinslow, *Resegregation as Curriculum*, xxxi; Austin, *Words*.

17 "Rather than identifying the discrete agents in the assemblage, we, as researchers attempting posthuman methodological practices, consider forces, vitalities, things, that act on and through vital materialities to produce the assemblage that we also become with/in. The implications for thinking what constitutes 'analysis,' or what is given weight in the doing of analysis, is no longer a relevant question. The question becomes how to attend to emergent and contingent forces." Jackson and Mazzei, "Posthuman Inquiry," 105.

18 Instead of exemplifying what we are thinking, "the encounter should serve as an example *to* thought . . . 'until a whole new system starts to form.'" Koczy quoting Massumi, *Beckett, Deleuze and Performance*, 85.

19 "What does it mean to disarticulate, to cease to be an organism? How can we convey how easy it is, and the extent to which we do it every day?" Deleuze and Guattari, *A Thousand Plateaus*, 159–160.

20 "There is also a performative aspect to our inquiries – a way in which the design of our inquiries – conceptually and materially – constitute the phenomena we study and they in return constitute us as subjects." Rosiek and Kinslow, *Resegregation as Curriculum*, xxvi.

Bibliography

Anzaldúa, Gloria. *Borderlands/La Frontera: The New Mestiza*. San Francisco: Aunt Lute, 1987.

Austin, John L. *How to Do Things with Words*. Oxford: Oxford University Press, 2009.

Butler, Judith. *Bodies That Matter: On the Discursive Limits of "Sex."* New York: Routledge, 1993.

Deleuze, Gilles, and Félix Guattari. *A Thousand Plateaus: Capitalism and Schizophrenia*. Translated by Brian Massumi. Minneapolis, MN: University of Minnesota Press, 1987.

Derrida, Jacques. *The Post Card: From Socrates to Freud and Beyond*. Translated by Alan Bass. Chicago, IL: University of Chicago Press, 1987.

———. *Archive Fever: A Freudian Impression*. Chicago, IL: University of Chicago Press, 1996.

Hayden, Patrick. *Multiplicity and Becoming: The Pluralist Empiricism of Gilles Deleuze*. New York: Peter Lang, 1998.

Jackson, Alecia Y., and Lisa A. Mazzei. "Thinking with an Agentic Assemblage in Posthuman Inquiry." In *Posthuman Research Practices in Education*, edited by Christina Hughes and Carol Ann Taylor, 93–107. New York: Palgrave Macmillan, 2016.

James, William. *Essays in Radical Empiricism; and a Pluralistic Universe*. Edited by Ralph Barton Perry. New York: E.P. Dutton, 1971.

———. *Pragmatism & the Meaning of Truth*. Cambridge, MA: Harvard University Press, 1978.

Koczy, Daniel. *Beckett, Deleuze and Performance: A Thousand Failures and a Thousand Inventions*. New York: Springer, 2018.

Lorde, Audre. *Sister Outsider: Essays and Speeches*. Berkeley, CA: Clarkson Potter/Ten Speed, 2012.

Malewski, Erik, and Nathalia Jaramillo. *Epistemologies of Ignorance in Education*. Charlotte, NC: IAP, 2011.

Minsky, Carly. "The Universe Is Made of Tiny Bubbles Containing Mini-Universes, Scientists Say." *Vice* (blog), October 24, 2019. www.vice.com/en_us/article/j5yngp/the-universe-is-made-of-tiny-bubbles-containing-mini-universes-scientists-say.

Rosiek, Jerry, and Kathy Kinslow. *Resegregation as Curriculum: The Meaning of the New Racial Segregation in U.S. Public Schools*. New York: Routledge, 2016. https://doi.org/10.4324/9781315748566.

Tillett, Wade. "Creating the Real." *Curriculum Inquiry* 41, no. 1 (January 1, 2011): 132–142. https://doi.org/10.1111/j.1467-873X.2010.00530.x.

Tillett, Wade, Daniel T. Barney, Nadine M. Kalin, Hector D. Lopez, Oren Ergas, Christopher Au, Heather McLeod, Maureen Ryan, and You Dear Reader. "A Readers' Rebellion." *Journal of Curriculum and Pedagogy* 16, no. 1 (2019): 97–114. https://doi.org/10.1080/15505170.2018.1525447.

Tuana, Nancy. "Coming to Understand: Orgasm and the Epistemology of Ignorance." *Hypatia* 19, no. 1 (2004): 194–232.

Acknowledgments

I suppose it is fitting for a book on disjunctions that I don't remember when the idea for this originally occurred to me. But I can say much progress was initially made in the fall of 2019 while I was on sabbatical. During that time and well beyond, Jenna Cushing-Leubner was a tireless reader, critic, and supporter.

Bill Schubert has been an unwavering mentor to me continuously since even before he chaired my dissertation committee – which resulted in a previous book, *Living the Questions: Dispatches From a Life Already in Progress*.

Alice Salt, from Routledge, not only found interest in this project but kindly supported me in revising numerous proposal drafts.

My family, from parents to grandparents to siblings, have been a source of inspiration for me – especially my children, Alvin, Brianna, and Brittney.

My mother-in-law, Karen Craig took great care in proofreading these pages.

My wife, Anne, has read and responded to countless drafts and donated unbelievable amounts of time and energy to supporting my own efforts.

Introduction

~

We lie. We slip. We hide. We omit. We forget. We ignore. We sleep. We start over. We skip past. We multitask.[1]

~

We are inscribed in our small pocket of awareness. We are overloaded and ignorant and lost in habit. Things slip by. Most things. We have a point of view, a horizon. We don't see most of the world around us. We are limited by our beliefs and past experiences and hardware as to what we are even able to see, even if it is right in front of us.

~

45 years × 365 days =
16,425 times of going to sleep
(of course higher than that including times of waking in the night, naps),
16,425 times of waking up

~

We have discontinuities in our daily life. We go to sleep. We wake up as if nothing happened. Our self, our conception of self, vanishes for a third of our life, and it is no big deal. We turn off and on, off and on.

~

We become awake. We become asleep.

These are not so much transitions as transformations.

From the exterior, one becomes a sleeper; but from the interior, one ceases to exist.

We ignore it daily, with faith that we will awake. It is "no big deal." And yet, as children, we sense something about going to sleep is enormous. The world will go on without us. There is no guarantee we will again exist. Lullabies and prayers. If I die before I wake . . .

~

DOI: 10.4324/ 9781003471882-1

Consider the amount that we forget, sleep, are distracted or overloaded, or more broadly are just ignorant or make assumptions. What is apparent is that most of our lives are gaps. We perceive and remember with a bucket full of holes. We are blind to the learned assumptions required for living a life.

How do we deal with the gaps? How could we not deal with the gaps? It's mostly gaps. We live in an abyss.

How do we *use* gaps? Gaps are built in as an integral part of all parts of living and learning. Gaps are essential to each concept, to perception, to memory.

~

Last night, it was very dark. It was raining, so the clouds covered any light from the stars or moon. Once my eyes adjusted, I could see areas of black that weren't quite as black as the rest of the black. Different textures of black. The textures I associated with the mound of blankets on my shoulders or hips, with the areas by the windows. I shut my eyes to go to sleep. I still saw the same textures in the same places. I opened, I shut. I touched my eyelids. Yes, shut. The textures remained.[2]

~

I want to take time to stop, listen, and wonder. To try to become aware of and really see the gaps and how I get through them.

~

What we are claiming is a collection of reals much more diverse than what is considered "objective." A radical empiricism, that is to say an actual empiricism, does not simply ignore the parts of experience that don't fit a model.[3]

We inhabit multiple worlds, multiple selves, multiple bodies. We travel through multiple dimensions.

~

We are taking William James's pluralism[4] seriously. What is it like to live through multiple worlds? Further, we are extending his pluralism to apply to the self. What is it like to live through multiple selves? How do these worlds and selves overlap? How do they remain separate?

Following Deleuze and Guattari, what is it like to see the self as an assemblage, as a part of an assemblage, as composed of assemblages? What is the experience of difference? We believe Deleuze and Guattari that "to disarticulate, to cease to be an organism," is experienced "every day."[5] What we have constructed here is a sort of poststructural phenomenology of these everyday disarticulations, a first-person accounting of the experience of these gaps. Pluralism and difference aren't just some theoretical constructs. We experience them every day right here in the course of our normal lives.

Further still, we discuss how we put those gaps to use. How, despite our (intentional) blindnesses to our own incompleteness, we actually leverage that incompleteness to our own advantage.

~

We should stop ignoring discontinuities in everyday life. We should notice and accept and even celebrate them. We should look at how we already navigate and leverage these disjunctions.[6] We should extend these methods. We don't expect to find anything completely new – sleep and forgetting are nothing new – though a life of fissures feels like a new postmodern condition. We are beginning in the middle. We have always already begun. Gaps are programmed into us, a fundamental part of who we are: sleep, heartbeats, birth and death, generations and revolutions and paradigm shifts.

~

"Thought . . . is always and already social."[7] Self is always and already social. Perception and reality are always and already social. Memory is always and already social. Feeling is always and already social. Gaps are always and already social. There is no direct access to a singular real. There is no objective view. We are constantly making it up, negotiating, refuting.

~

The partial observer is not only partial in themself but partial also because the set of facts themself is partial.[8] Wholeness is an illusion,[9] a failure to examine the constraints of truth, the assumptions of a whole, the limits and borders and even the ground itself as a system.

~

Each real has, baked within it, exclusions, economies, exchanges, inequities, and injustices. As certain realities are pushed forward, the inequities magnify, the rules of exchange become more ubiquitous. It is pointless to call for justice without changing the real.

Justice also has at its base a rule of law – an economy of exchange – a singular real.

~

How dare I say this when leaders openly combat the truth? Because they are only trying to impose the tyranny of another truth. How dare I say this when justice has not been served? Justice is never served. It relies on an economy, an exchange value, which can never hold because so much is lost, so much can never be restored. Exchange value, reality, self are exactly what further themselves as they are inseparable from power.[10]

~

Our condition is not new. We've always been trying to pick up the pieces, bridge the discontinuities, assume and believe and have faith.

Perhaps what is new is the ineffectiveness of our culture to provide a holistic worldview, a holistic life story.

There have always been mysteries. Cracks.

To look at these cracks might reveal something else, might lead to a new way of understanding self, world, life. We are so good at looking past so many disjunctions. We have habits and customs to deal with them that we so often deploy without thinking, without a care or worry.

~

Reality is much more complicated than we were led to believe. In some ways, the assumptions we make are necessary. But what this book seeks to uncover are assumptions we make yet hide from ourselves as unimportant or excluded – from the real, from the lived, from the self, from the world. Here, we look at how we use these assumptions, in large part unconsciously, to construct a singular lived experience – one life, one self, one world, while simultaneously we repeatedly violate that singular to our advantage (we hope). By looking at the exclusions and how they are constructed, we believe we can open new avenues, metaphors, and stories of life and the real. And by looking at how we use these exclusions, we expand our conscious range of strategies and invite new applications and constructions. To say it in a few words, by looking at the definitions of experience, their exclusions and the use of those exclusions, we hope to open ourselves to the expansive realities that we are already living. We hope to multiply the real.

This is not only important at the level of personal experience. Personal experience cannot be meaningfully separated from the social. I do not intend to say that the experience of gaps presented here is universal. The experience of gaps, even the existence of gaps, depends on culture, beliefs, personality. This project is limited by particularly situated thoughts, strategies, experiences, cultures, beliefs, personalities.

This is an expansion beyond a narrative of the singular and the continuous – beyond Truth and History.[11] It is to reposition experience as multiple and disjointed and to celebrate the resulting conflicts and opportunities. Ultimately, new worlds will arise out of the old ones, from the fractures. This is an exploration of those fractures. They are already here. They always have been. They always will be. And we would be wise to embrace them in a more conscious manner if we are able. This is the great hope of this project: that there can be new reals, and that they are already with us – sprouting. Some, even, fully grown.

~

That we can unlearn how to stitch together, paste over, conjoin.[12]

~

That we can and do leverage the fractures of our lives.[13] That disjunctures are opportunities, insulators, cracks, new beginnings, fissures, and tentative movements.

~

We hope to point out the slippages by which freedom is enacted, however large or small. We note how we transfer between multiple dimensions. How we inhabit multiple modes. How life is always a step ahead of us, escaping. We don't think we will ever catch up, but perhaps we can be more conscious of this gap between living and lived, of how ingenious we are.

This is not to excuse the prevailing real but rather to show that sprouting within it are thousands more. We do not believe we can use logic against itself. We do not believe we can restore what is lost. Instead, we hope to understand how to travel between reals, between exclusions, in order to avoid being pinned down. And, to our great relief, we realize we are always already doing this – searching the crevices. While in one real we are crucified, in another, we are arisen.

~

Notes

1 "But just as definitely is [the world] is *not* one . . . there is no species of connexion which will not fail, if, instead of choosing conductors for it, you choose non-conductors. You are then arrested at your very first step and have to write the world down as a pure many from that particular point of view. If our intellect had been as much interested in disjunctive as it is in conjunctive relations, philosophy would have equally successfully celebrated the world's *disunion.*" Em in original. James, *Pragmatism*, 68.

2 To get at the wholeness of reality, the concreteness, the movement, you need to "place your self . . . inside of the living, moving, active thickness of the real . . ." James summarizing Bergson, *A Pluralistic Universe*, 247. "The pluralist, James argues, starts with the 'each' instead of the 'all,' with the particular experience and its context of relations, rather than an absolute whole or totalizing system." Brians, *Empiricism and Multiplicity*. "In the ethno-poetics and performance of the shaman, my people, the Indians, did not split the artistic from the functional, the sacred from the secular, art from everyday life." Anzaldua, *Borderlands / La Frontera*, 66.

3 "For the radical empiricist, the world is best understood as a complex network of pluralistic collections or compositions, since some parts of it are related and some are not, or are related only indirectly through a network of intermediary relationships. The view of unity put forth by a radical empiricism is the dissolution of a single absolute Unity into a diffuse network of differentiated unities or multiplicities that are incomplete, partial, and continuously transforming." Processes creating these are pluralistic. Hayden, *Multiplicity and Becoming*, 89. "For the radical empiricist, the world is dynamic, partial – that is, it cannot be completely unified all at once – and constantly changing. . . . We experience the pluralism of the world within ourselves and we continually act upon, invent, and create new versions of existence out of this multiplicity." Hayden, *Multiplicity and Becoming*, 90.

4 James, *A Pluralistic Universe*.

5 Deleuze and Guattari, *A Thousand Plateaus*, 159–160.

6 "Life does not proceed by the association and addition and elements, but by dissociation and division." Bergson, *Creative Evolution*, 89.

7 Middleton and Brown summarizing Halbwachs, *Experience*, 8.

8 Not a "relativity of truth but . . . a truth of the relative." Deleuze and Guattari, *What Is Philosophy*, 130.

9 "Is negation as the structure of the judicative proposition at the origin of nothingness? Or on the contrary is nothingness as the structure of the real, the origin and

foundation of negation?" Sartre, *Being and Nothingness*, 7. "There is nothing in heaven or on earth which does not contain in itself being and nothingness." Hegel, Greater Logic, qtd. in Sartre, *Being and Nothingness*, 13.

10 Foucault, *Discipline and Punish*.

11 "Rather than 'lock in' on singular truths and right translations, epistemologies of ignorance illustrate that within the original truth there is continuous movement and transformation, an uncertainty that opens towards a myriad of disjunctive interpretations and incommensurable truths." Malewski and Jaramillo, *Ignorance*, 11.

12 "But on both sides, philosophy and science (like art itself with its third side) include an *I do not know* that has become positive and creative, the condition of creation itself, and consists in determining *by* what one does not know . . ." Deleuze and Guattari, *What Is Philosophy*, 128.

13 "[I]n our general dealings with the world of influences, we now need conductors and now need non-conductors and wisdom lies in knowing which is which at the appropriate moment." James, *Pragmatism*, 68.

Bibliography

Anzaldúa, Gloria. *Borderlands/La Frontera: The New Mestiza*. San Francisco: Aunt Lute, 1987.

Bergson, Henri. *Creative Evolution*. Translated by Arthur Mitchell. Mineola, NY: Dover, 1998.

Brians, Ella. *Empiricism and Multiplicity in the Work of Gilles Deleuze*. University of Warwick, 2006. https://warwick.ac.uk/fac/soc/philosophy/news/archive/continental-empiricism/schedule/brians/.

Deleuze, Gilles, and Félix Guattari. *A Thousand Plateaus: Capitalism and Schizophrenia*. Translated by Brian Massumi. Minneapolis, MN: University of Minnesota Press, 1987.

———. *What Is Philosophy?* New York: Columbia University Press, 1994.

Foucault, Michel. *Discipline and Punish: The Birth of the Prison*. Translated by A Sheridan. 2nd Vintage Books ed. New York: Vintage Books, 1995.

Hayden, Patrick. *Multiplicity and Becoming: The Pluralist Empiricism of Gilles Deleuze*. New York: Peter Lang, 1998.

James, William. *Essays in Radical Empiricism; and a Pluralistic Universe*. Edited by Ralph Barton Perry. New York: E.P. Dutton, 1971.

———. *Pragmatism & the Meaning of Truth*. Cambridge, MA: Harvard University Press, 1978.

Malewski, Erik, and Nathalia Jaramillo. *Epistemologies of Ignorance in Education*. Charlotte, NC: IAP, 2011.

Middleton, David, and Steve D. Brown. *The Social Psychology of Experience: Studies in Remembering and Forgetting*. London: Sage, 2005.

Sartre, Jean-Paul. *Being and Nothingness*. Avenel, NJ: Gramercy Books, 1994.

Part I

Escaping Through Fractures

1 Lose

~

Lottery is the new religion. It allows you to hope there is a life beyond this one. At Grandfather's funeral, my brother said this life is not enough. My wife and I, we painted the dining room. We moved the fish tank. I painted the bare spot suddenly evident.

My life was enough a long time ago. Now, it just keeps going. I'm not complaining. Buying that ticket is a defeat.

Last night, I sat on my son's fishing boat, on the trailer, in the sea of grass and soybeans behind my house. I imagined building something there. I imagined turning all those fields into wildflowers. When I win the lotto, I thought. It's raining tonight, or else I'd sit on the boat on the trailer.

There are soybeans and corn in rows. Perpendicular roads with perpendicular poles. Power lines sagging between. They buzz and hiss. The grass is cut. It is all carefully maintained, as far as the eye can see.

They put green AstroTurf around the hole. As if to hide the dirt. They didn't seem to want to lower him down, but my grandma waited, insistent.

The groundskeeper had on a tie. He accidentally dropped the crank handle under the casket. He ran to get the vise grips. He raised the dead. No use burying a perfectly good handle. We waited. We understood.

My daughter took a photo of the sides of dirt. We wondered where was the dirt that goes on top. There wasn't any to throw on. Thud. Like in the movies. It is all carefully maintained so that we won't see.

~

We bought broilers. We raised them in a triangular cage. We moved it when there was too much shit on the ground. They were stupid birds. Bred to grow fat and fast. They barely moved.

The first one squawked and struggled against the killing cone. I raised the knife. I slit its throat. The blood poured out. Onto the dirt and weeds next to the tree trunk. Not as much as you would think.

I'd cleaned the stainless steel table with the hose with some bleach. I sliced the skin from ass to neck. I pulled out their guts. I cut off their heads. I cut

DOI: 10.4324/ 9781003471882-3

off their feet. I cut off their wings. I turned their skin inside out one by one. I peeled it off. I discarded the feathers. Their bodies were warm on my hands. I sprayed them off with the hose. I put them in gallon Ziploc bags, one each. Meat. Most of them went to the freezer. We had one for supper. Chicken and noodles. My daughter found a small feather. She didn't eat any more.

~

At Grandpa's funeral, my brother said this life is not enough. God is a hope that belittles. Like the lotto.

At some point, life was enough. That was a sin. Now it just keeps going. Save the receipts.

They put AstroTurf around the hole. To hide the dirt. They didn't lower him. Grandma waited, insistent.

The groundskeeper dropped the handle. He ran to get the vise grips. The casket came up. No use burying a perfectly good handle.

~

We give loss a purpose. Loss becomes necessary. Loss becomes part of an economy, a trade. We look in to the abyss. Now, it has our function. We send things in. We extract things out. Loss serves a purpose. Loss is mastered.

On the stone table, we raise the knife.

We sacrifice. We offer up an unrecoverable. Death becomes a gift that works backward toward life.

Our sins are removed. Our plodding and difficult moments are rewarded. Our life is ensured through a planned and unnecessary death. A piece of ourselves is given. Something of value is revoked. We beat death at death. We are destroyers, not just the destroyed. We plan an abyss. We contain it.

We create absence. We protect ourselves. We create an order to the world. Loss is not for us anytime soon. Loss is not eternal. Loss is bound, through purpose and ritual. Constrained, limited, unfinished, incomplete.

The abyss remains.

~

My brother said this life is not enough. God is a hope that belittles.

At some point, life was enough. That was a sin.

They put AstroTurf around the hole. They didn't lower him. Grandma waited.

The groundskeeper dropped the handle. The casket came up.

~

I control death by imparting it. I give what cannot be given. I receive what cannot be received. I put to an end. I avoid my own.

This gap is eternal. Death is bottomless. So are its reversed potentials. Sacrifice trades it, economizes it, requires it. Loss is no longer loss. Control is transferred. Into the abyss. Out of the abyss. I am a sinner. I crucify. I am forgiven. I am eternal. An abyss turned inside out. I offer up an undeserved death. I mortalize the immortal.

Into the Ziploc bag.

~

Life is not enough. God assures us.

Life is enough. That is a sin.

They didn't lower him. Grandma waited.

~

I swat the fly so it will no longer buzz. I trap the mouse so it will no longer chew. So many endings with so little thought. Loss is not necessarily magnificent. It is so common. It goes unnoticed most of the time.

~

Grandma waited.

~

I cannot give up loss. Loss is important. Loss is the last part of what's lost. Loss is all that's left.

Memory does not exist without that sense of loss, without a time past, without a difference between what is now and what was then.

Our sins are forgiven, not forgotten.

Loss is a fundamental state of the world.[1] Moment by moment, time passes.

Almost all is lost. Most of the rest is loss.

~

Grandma waits.

~

Note

1 "The ultimate evil in the temporal world is deeper than any specific evil. It lies in the fact that the past fades, that time is a 'perpetual perishing' [Locke]. Objectification involves elimination. . . . process entails loss." Whitehead, *Process and Reality*, 401.

Bibliography

Whitehead, Alfred North. *Process and Reality: An Essay in Cosmology*. Edited by David Ray Griffin and Donald W. Sherburne. Corrected ed. Gifford Lectures 1927–1928. New York: Free Press, 1978.

2 Escape

Past the railroad lines. Down the lane. Up the stairs. Through the attic. Out the window. Suspended. Snow-dusted fields. The antenna tower. The rattling of the pane. The humming of the space heater. The clacking of the keys. A place twice removed or more.

It was crowded. The exposed insulation. The rolled-up carpets. The card table with a leg broken off. The holes in the floor.

I hauled out the carpets, the table. I covered the holes. I put up two pieces of plywood.

I rubbed in the tung oil. Rich. Deep. I washed the plaster walls, the ceiling. Wildly mottled. A modernist monochrome.

I remake this room again each time I rub it down.[1] Each time I sit.

I rebuild this room empty. A plot to escape.

~

My bones are pinned down, immovable. Just beyond is the surface. I resist rising. Here, I am safe. Comfortable. Invisible. Nonexistent. Unaccountable. Free.

I resist knowing what I have escaped, as then my escape will be over. There is no escape. Only escaping.

Sometimes, I hear the sounds – without the labels. They wash into me, soak to my marrow, reverberating. A low rumble. A high-pitched hiss. A buzz. A whir.

This state is free. This state is hard to inhabit. I feel the freedom. The comfort. The warmth. The safety. I am to be left alone, please. I am forming. A half-baked loaf. Awareness without being aware. Life without speech or body or obligation. A pulsing and a feeling. Without borders or objects or shadows. A yellowish haze.

I've tried to develop a prescription for this space. Directions for entering. Drugs or rituals or certain times of day. Mostly, it eludes me. Until it does not. Until I happen upon it. How long do I inhabit this placeless place, this bodiless body? It doesn't matter. Time does not pass. This is momentary eternity. Seconds. Hours. Days. Only someone on the outside could tell; that wouldn't really tell anything.

DOI: 10.4324/ 9781003471882-4

Sometimes, I don't bother to try to inhabit this. I am happy just to bypass and be gone. Disconnected. Unwired. Closed. Internal. Absent. Asleep.

~

I heard the snap. It didn't sound as sharp as I expected. Maybe a mouse softened, absorbed its blow.

The life insurance came. They took my blood. They said no. I wonder what they know that I don't.

I wonder how I'm going to die. Probably Alzheimer's. That's what I have always feared. I see early indicators.

Grandpa didn't recognize me. He did the next morning. I went to visit him on his deathbed. Propped up so he could look out the window at the river. The cottage, open rafters, a place to store the skis, a concrete-block boathouse, an aluminum pier. He built it all. The river floods the cottage. Deposits the silt across the concrete floor, in each crevice between the wood floorplate and studs. They tried to condemn it; my father tells me smiling: I told them they have to look at it. When they did, when they saw how each surface was cleaned. They said, "Oh, you are right. We never expected. We definitely don't have to condemn this."

The river is washing over me. There is no struggle. I am resolved. I do not plead. I want to die at peace in the rushing water. I hope I won't panic.

I folded my clothes neatly. I placed them on my shoes. I swam out away from the abandoned mine. I passed the edge of the cliff. I resolved. I will swim until the end.

I turned back.

~

I still can't sleep. She has gotten up and gone to the restroom twice now. She can't sleep either. I hear her breathing. I hear my breathing.

I hear the rushing of the river.

~

Note

1 Bachelard, *Poetics of Space*, 67.

Bibliography

Bachelard, Gaston. *The Poetics of Space*. Translated by Maria Jolas. Boston: Beacon Press, 1969.

3 Break

The rotifer was in the permafrost for 24,000 years. Suspended. It resumed. The pause was over. 24,000 years was the blink of an eye, no different from a catnap. It simply waited. Until.

~

Discontinuity is an ancient strategy.[1] Life stops. New life proliferates. Variates. Mutates. Individual life is finite. Reproduction is exponential.

Today is a new day. We live it differently than yesterday. The dendrites rewire themselves. In between, we wait for the sunlight. Until.

Consciousness is recreated. Suspended then taken up again. Destroyed but rising again.

What we take to be the inner experience, the self, is not passed on. There is much passed on. Continuity and discontinuity are wrapped together. There are pauses. Increases and decreases. A line where life expands and contracts. Repeatedly. Differently.

~

The sugar cube takes its own time to dissolve.[2] We must wait.

~

There are so many worlds. They can't be inhabited all at once. They refuse to be bound into one. The worlds are larger than us. They contain other things. They contain other people. We enter into different bodies. We enter into different reals. Sometimes, we translate something between worlds. Sometimes, we are left to piece together what happened without us. Worlds may go on with or without us. There are overlaps. There are places you can't get to. Reality is made of the "each" rather than the "all."[3]

~

There we are.

We see ourselves on the screen. We are there. We are here. Memory doubles over.

DOI: 10.4324/ 9781003471882-5

I see myself transmitted. I see myself retransmitted.

Image of image. Sound of sound. Body of body. All the way down.

~

I speak this into my phone in the middle of the forest in the snow, alone. Communication is deferred.

~

I step in deep fresh snow. I sink to a float. A posthole. Again. Again. The same tracks become smoother, easier, a compacted slot to walk and drag the sled. Deer tracks follow along. They float deeper.

~

Mathematical thought is a way to leap gaps. Mathematical thought is a way to unify perceptions.[4] Object permanence, space, location, time, categories, language – all theorize perceptions as parts of conceptual wholes.

Let us conceptualize other wholes. Let us replace time. Let us replace space.

Let us stop conceptualizing wholes. Let us see tentative. Let us see partial. Let us see local.

~

Collective gaps are not separate from personal gaps. Subjectivity is socially constructed. We inhabit revolutions. We inhabit paradigm shifts. We inhabit changing discourses.

~

I keep the secret. The secret is a partial gap. The secret is a gap of access. Those who know the secret are aware there is a gap for those who don't know. Those who don't know the secret are not aware there is a secret. There is no gap.

~

Gaps can last a second or a billion years. Within those gaps are gaps.[5]

~

There is no beforelife.[6] We come from nowhere.

~

When pressed, I responded with a simple, "I don't remember."[7]

~

Forgiveness leaves the gap. Forgiveness bridges the gap. A submerged debt.

~

Erase. Edit.

~

I lie. I intentionally construct a discontinuity. I create an alternative continuity. I short-circuit the continuity of experience. I create a new story. I leave out critical elements. There are gaps. I fill these gaps. I erase the gaps. I mislead. I distract. I create an opening. I create an alternate real. I create an escape.

~

My grandpa showed me how you freeze a small tub of water, then you place a penny on it. If the penny is on the bottom, that means the freezer thawed.

My daughter took a time-lapse video of herself sleeping.

Ankle bracelets trip an alarm if the wearer wanders outside of the geofence.

The top of the canning lid pops when the seal is broken.

~

We attempt to make gaps visible. Gaps exist all around us. They open without a trace. They close without a trace. We are not aware there is a gap in our knowledge. We assume continuity. There is discontinuity. Things happen while we sleep. We prefer that they don't. We pretend that they don't. If the food has spoiled often enough, we attempt to build in safeguards, tripwires, alerts. Warning: the continuity has been broken. Unknown things happened. Eat at your own risk. Botulism.

These are not foolproof. These are not 100%.

Doubt persists.

~

Stop transmitting your signal. Wrap your electronic device in plastic wrap then aluminum foil. Repeat a few times.

~

The perforation is a line of weakness. It controls the future break.

The wind chime is a composition of preselected notes. It randomly composes a melody.

The trail is an opening in the undergrowth. It influences the paths of future animals. It reinforces itself.

~

Naming things is a way to contain them. It aids in seeing something as an object, as delimited, as closed and whole.

~

Walking the pedway is an architectural montage. Through each door is a new world. No transitions. A path of openings.[8]

~

I am lost.

~

I forget where I am, what I am doing. Force of habit. I remove myself. Without intending to, I make myself absent from this present. I fall into the daydream. Reveries.

When I become aware of where I am again, I look for clues. I try to reestablish my bearings, the timeline. The washcloth is a hint. It is in my hand. I think back. I definitely remember putting soap on it. But whether or not I rinsed, I don't know. I do the only rational thing. I rinse. Perhaps again. I double back. I retrace where I left off. Perhaps I cover the same ground. It is a way to be sure, to cover that tiny gap – to amend a process in one mode that got lost while engaging in another. I jump back and forth. The progress is not linear. I pick up again and again. Mostly, I don't notice. That is just how life is. A series of jolts and transportations. A protocol that sends back what it received and looks for missing instances. I live double.

~

Notes

1 One of the "categories of existence" is "Multiplicities, or Pure Disjunctions of Diverse Entities." Whitehead, *Process and Reality*, 26.
2 Bergson, *Creative Evolution*, 9.
3 James, *A Pluralistic Universe*, 138. "Now we are bringing earth to heaven." Prigogine and Stengers, *Order Out of Chaos*, 306. "For the movements of faith must constantly be made by virtue of the absurd, yet in such a way, be it observed, that one does not lose the finite but gains it every inch." Kierkegaard, *Fear and Trembling*, 48.
4 Tillett, "Mathematical Beings."
5 Gorvett, "Missing Billion Years."
6 In my Protestant upbringing, beforelife was never addressed.
7 "Put simply, saying something like, 'I don't remember' is a good way for speakers to leave options open in the conversation." Middleton and Brown, *Experience*, 90.
8 Inspired by the Chicago Pedway.

Bibliography

Bergson, Henri. *Creative Evolution*. Translated by Arthur Mitchell. Mineola, NY: Dover, 1998.

Gorvett, Zaria. "The Strange Race to Track Down a Missing Billion Years." *BBC*, September 1, 2021. www.bbc.com/future/article/20210901-the-strange-race-to-track-down-a-missing-billion-years.

James, William. *Essays in Radical Empiricism; and a Pluralistic Universe*. Edited by Ralph Barton Perry. New York: E.P. Dutton, 1971.

Kierkegaard, Søren. *Fear and Trembling*. Translated by W. Lowrie. Princeton, NJ: Princeton University Press, 1974.

Middleton, David, and Steve D. Brown. *The Social Psychology of Experience: Studies in Remembering and Forgetting*. London: Sage, 2005.

Prigogine, Ilya, and Isabelle Stengers. *Order Out of Chaos: Man's New Dialogue with Nature*. London: Heinemann, 1984.

Tillett, Wade. "We Are Mathematical Beings." *Qualitative Inquiry* 28, no. 3–4 (March 1, 2022): 396–402. https://doi.org/10.1177/10778004211059236.

Whitehead, Alfred North. *Process and Reality: An Essay in Cosmology*. Edited by David Ray Griffin and Donald W. Sherburne. Corrected ed. Gifford Lectures 1927–1928. New York: Free Press, 1978.

Part II

Reclaiming What Is Lost

4 Conjure

~

Grandpa was going to guide paying fishermen up through the lakes in Minnesota.

There were daughters to raise. There were bills to pay. There was a factory.

He bought a plot of land on the Tippecanoe River.

He built the cottage by hand.

The ice jams rose over the steps he formed. Over the live well with the spring eternally running. Over the pipe drain keeping the water high enough for this days' haul of bass and cats.

The door on the motor house is marked with the flood waters each season – a dash and a date.

What of the dam, what of the encroaching neighbors, what of a wilderness parceled out and riverbanks turned in to concrete?

We would laugh as the boats raced into the submerged rock in front because they didn't know.

The cottage walls ended at the rafters. Grandpa would throw his swim trunks over, inevitably ending in the butter dish. He would yell I don't remember what. But it was hilarious. Shared.

We had the wet guts on the plywood. We had the plastic 5-gallon bucket. We dug a hole for offal and heads under the pines where the mushrooms grow.

~

If I remember correctly.

~

To remember, we must forget.

~

I used to dream of the path through the woods.

I still dream of the path through the woods.

I can still conjure it up.

DOI: 10.4324/ 9781003471882-7

There are raspberries. The mornings with the sand. The morning with the sticky air.

The grass is high. The brush is dense.

The limb dips down. I climb it. I am perched. I hear the cows.

My mother has a garden. There are snakes. I cut the heads off with the blade of the shovel.

It is a whole universe.

Now the undergrowth is cut flat. The fields impinge. Threaten.

~

The path is gone as it was but exists as it never was. I don't bother to reach for it. It is there, in a box I don't open.

~

To conjure, we use the loss.[1] Not just the loss of memory but the loss at the heart of things. We cannot separate out a real and a remembered, a world and a perception, a fact and a feeling.[2] We cannot separate out a remembrance and a forgettance.[3] To conjure is to ride the border[4] of order and disorder.[5]

~

Remember our first year of marriage when we would walk to Pizza King – the low ceilings, the dark lights? That particular smell of our bathroom – something growing behind the walls?

Beside the low dresser, the one we stripped in the backyard, was you in something cotton early night.

Time loops back an empty cylinder with bumps reverberating hollow and whole.

The dog jumped through the screen and it ran right past me at you.

You outran it home.

~

If I am not mistaken.

~

Remember our first year of marriage when we would go to your grandparents' house for dinner once a week for the best meals we had that year? Your grandparents all to ourselves? Remember the breakfast nook with the windows along two sides and the sun that would come in?

The semis would barrel past our house and wake you up, but I would sleep soundly beside you. Always feeling safe.

The dog jumped through the screen. You stayed back to distract him and sacrificed yourself. When he ran past you, you believed in me that I could outrun him home.[6]

~

Maybe.[7]

~

The cabin is deep in on the two-track logging roads. It sits within the pines and the maples and the poplars. There are duck lakes. There is a river. There is a valley. There is a bluff that overlooks it all. The world seems largely flat. Suddenly, it opens out. We see over the tops of the trees we inhabit.

I don't make it there as often as I would like. I have dreams to live there. A writer's life. Splitting wood and typing on the Underwood. Drinking whisky and cleaning fish. Those dreams are wrapped up with it. That secluded place in the woods, it is enough that it is there. That it exists. I carry it with me. A reserve, a refuge, a heaven. There, I go where things are right. I go there daily. Unspoiled. It exists beyond the actual.[8]

~

I nurture the memory.[9] I nurture the dream.

~

Somewhere before the house of my childhood was another house, with a staircase forever tall and steep, a railing overlooking at the top. I would come down at night when I smelled the popcorn. They thought I was asleep.

~

Or so I am told.[10]

~

There are only the stairs for me, vague but large.[11] It was a time before memory, the prehistory of my own life. It exists in plain sight, but I cannot see. It exists, outside of me, before me, a house, an unremembered womb. A step on the way to awareness, consciousness, self-narrative. I point to. I deduce. I believe. I imagine-remember – a fuzzy feeling or a foggy detail jutting out. A sort of pier in the haze of horizonless water. I tell the stories about the midnight popcorn, but somehow, those stories came from outside me. I am told the stories about the midnight popcorn. I try to square it with my memory, with myself. It remains stubbornly foreign. Here is a story about myself. I can connect it with the stairs. Not really. There is this life I don't remember people say is mine. I am told I grew continuously. I am told it is connected. I am told it is me. The experience is exterior. Childhood is an amalgamation of photos and stories and visits back. It is a disconnected jumble of partial moments, the beginnings of memories – a vague feeling that something is there, was there. I attempt to claim it. It remains elusive.

~

My bearded father is coming out of my parents' bedroom. I am scared. He tells me my great-grandfather has died. He has gotten burned burning the fencerow. Pneumonia.

I killed a rabbit on his land. It was coming up the other side of the gravel pit. Little wisps of dust as the shot hit the ground in a cloud. Grandpa showed me how to break the bladder. He held it by the head. He hit it on the ground. He hit it on the ground again. The guts dumped.

My great grandfather would rest in his chair with his hand out by his side, holding a pocketknife. When he relaxed enough that the pocketknife fell out and hit the floor, he would get up.[12]

~

Notes

1 Thus, not only is memory actively constructed socially, so is what is not. Collective forgetting is literally written out of (by destruction, curation, taboo, rules, etc.) the places and artifacts in and through which the group dwells. Just as memory is actively managed socially, so is forgetting. In fact, to speak of memory and forgetting as two separate activities belies the fact that they are both parts of the same activity. To select, to curate (to do curriculum, *currere*), to live is to do both simultaneously. The photograph and the home movie have the frame, the point of view, the exposure length, the moment selected. The object is used in particular ways for particular activities by particular people. The diary or memoire or letter selects certain actions conveyed in certain words. Forgetting (as is remembering) is so often cast as a particular failure of an individual's mind to recall. In truth, forgetting is as active as it is passive, as intentional as it is a failure, and at least as collective as it is individual (besides, there is no dichotomy between individual and collective – they mutually create each other). Forgetting is an important part of the active management of the collective and the individual, the group and the self. Middleton and Brown, *Experience*.

2 "Recollection, for the Betsimisaraka, is not an abstract cognitive act, but, rather, occurs in a 'fuzzy space between thinking and feeling,' as a 'feeling memory.'" Cole quoted in Middleton and Brown, *Experience*, 26.

3 "*Too much remembering actually makes us less able to know* or to hold on to experiences such that they can stand out as meaningful." Acampora, "Forgetting the Subject," 50.

4 Like Latour describes in *We Have Never Been Modern*, there is a dual act of purification where the memory is constructed as a pure other, and the fact of that construction is covered over, forgotten. Memory is constructed as if it is objective, accurate (or at least a true representation of a subjective experience) – as if it is filed away (as with Derrida's archive), but the decisions as to the active reconstruction, re-membering, (as to the storage, retrieval, and interpretation in the archive) are looked past, covered over, "forgotten." *Lethe* (Greek etymological root for forgetting) suggests covering; "to forget is to bury" because we can't look at it or are done with it. Hyde, *Forgetting*, 50. The *Archive Fever* (Derrida) occurs also at the level of personal recollection to the degree we forget or turn a blind eye to our own selection and (re-)construction.

5 The active pattern making cascade in the brain is always working (at least in some modes, like conscious perception). The brain operates near the tipping/critical point, in a quasi-critical state. "[L]ocalized episodes of disordered brain activity, like avalanches in a sand pile, help keep the overall system in healthy balance. . . . a system is perfectly balanced between order and disorder, according to Plenz." Ouellette, "Model Mind."

6 These three paragraphs written by Anne Tillett.

7 Memory of the same evening is different because we "care to know different things." Bolles, *Remembering and Forgetting*, 243.

8 "The true paradise is the paradise that we have lost." Proust quoted in Hyde, *Forgetting*, 308.

9 "Remembering is an act of imagination. . . . Remembering is a creative, constructive process." Bolles, *Remembering and Forgetting*, XI. "When we understand memory as a constructive power, we also see how vitally and creatively we confront daily

life with our whole being." Bolles, *Remembering and Forgetting*, XII. "Memory is a living product of desire, attention, insight, and consciousness." Bolles, *Remembering and Forgetting*, XIV. Bartlett quoted: "We mingle interpretation with description, interpolate things not originally present, transform without effort and without knowledge . . . In a world of constantly changing environment, literal recall is extraordinarily unimportant." Middleton and Brown, *Experience*, 18. "[W]e must think of remembering and forgetting as a creative process that is entirely coextensive with the novelty and change of our unfolding durations." Middleton and Brown, *Experience*, 221.

10 "Halbwachs viewed memory as an intrinsically social process. Not only is the form remembering takes shaped by the collective, but the very content of any given memory is also, Halbwachs argued, a social product." Middleton and Brown, *Experience*, 3.

11 "He experiences the house in its reality and in its virtuality, by means of thought and dreams. . . . Through dreams, the various dwelling-places in our lives co-penetrate and retain the treasure of former days." Bachelard, *Poetics of Space*, 5. "Memories of the outside world will never have the same tonality as those of home, and, by recalling these memories, we add to our store of dreams; we are never real historians, but always near poets, and our emotion is perhaps nothing but an expression of a poetry that was lost. / Thus by approaching the house images with care not to break up the solidarity of memory and imaginations, we may hope to make others feel all the psychological elasticity of an image that moves us to unimaginable depth. . . . [I]f I were asked to name the chief benefit of the house, I should say: the house shelters daydreaming, the house protects the dreamer, the house allows one to dream in peace." Bachelard, *Poetics of Space*, 6.

12 My history is "what I shall have been for what I am in the process of becoming." Lacan quoted in Smith, "Forgetting to Remember," 108.

Bibliography

Acampora, Christa Davis. "Forgetting the Subject." In *Reading Nietzsche at the Margins*, edited by Steven V. Hicks and Alan Rosenberg, 34–56. West Lafayette, IN: Purdue University Press, 2008.

Bachelard, Gaston. *The Poetics of Space*. Translated by Maria Jolas. Boston: Beacon Press, 1969.

Bolles, Edmund Blair. *Remembering and Forgetting: An Inquiry into the Nature of Memory*. New York: Walker and Co, 1988.

Derrida, Jacques. *Archive Fever: A Freudian Impression*. Chicago, IL: University of Chicago Press, 1996.

Hyde, Lewis. *A Primer for Forgetting: Getting Past the Past*. New York: Farrar, Straus and Giroux, 2019.

Latour, Bruno. *We Have Never Been Modern*. Translated by C. Porter. Cambridge, MA: Harvard University Press, 1993.

Middleton, David, and Steve D. Brown. *The Social Psychology of Experience: Studies in Remembering and Forgetting*. London: Sage, 2005.

Ouellette, Jennifer. "A Fundamental Theory to Model the Mind." *Quanta Magazine*, April 3, 2014. www.quantamagazine.org/toward-a-theory-of-self-organized-criticality-in-the-brain-20140403/.

Smith, Kathleen White. "Forgetting to Remember: Anamnesis and History in J. M. G. Le Clézio's Desert." *Studies in 20th & 21st Century Literature* 10, no. 1 (September 1, 1985). https://doi.org/10.4148/2334-4415.1176.

5 Exceed

I am standing on a hill outside the door of the butcher. I have my arm around my cow. We are talking. She is explaining that she is starting to understand fractions. She still has trouble with proportions. I am intrigued.

People are walking by in the fairgrounds with their cows. Some have been sold. Some have gone before us to the butcher. There is offal on the asphalt beneath our feet. I kick it out of the way with my boot. I hope my cow doesn't notice.

We continue to wait for the butcher. I am starting to doubt whether I should eat cows. It seems like if they can talk and do fractions, maybe that is cruel.

My cow suddenly seems to realize what is through that door. She charges through, tossing her head. They put her down.

~

There is not a strict separation between perceiving, remembering, dreaming, imagining. All involve gaps and leaps. All involve conjuring. All involve excess that bleeds in to other modes.

~

I remember, now that I am telling the story, they texted to say to come pick up the beef. In the next 2 days, please. Our freezers are full.

~

Between modes, some things are lost and some things are gained.

~

I am driving to Rio, Wisconsin. It is an hour and a half away, but it is beautiful outside. I've got the top and doors off the jeep. The Styrofoam coolers are stacked and ratcheted down in the back. I get there and give her my name. She says it will be at least 10 minutes. I stand by the counter. She comes back. She tells me it will be at least 10 minutes. I stand by the counter. I watch the guys mingling around the little bar. They call someone over to them. The someone serves them samples. They drink. It will be 10 minutes, she says. I finally take the hint. I start wandering around the store – whiskeys and meats and cheeses.

DOI: 10.4324/ 9781003471882-8

They bring out the frozen beef. It sounds like billiard balls. It is frozen so solid. They are plastic wrapped with printed labels. Usually, it is butcher paper with stamps. This place is fancy. You can see the deep red of the beef.

I write two checks – one for the butcher and one for the farmer. $150 and $450.

~

All modes have excess. Gaps can overflow.

~

When I get home, I stack the three coolers with the beef in them on top of each other on a digital scale in the basement. It is 118 pounds. The Styrofoam can't weigh much of that. It was about $600. A little over $5 a pound. Not bad for these times. My wife looks at some hamburger we got from the grocery in the fridge. $5.99 a pound. What we got includes roasts and prime rib. I feel better.

We empty the freezer mostly. We put the beef in some heavy plastic bags with handles to organize it. A freezer that turns over so you can put the new beef on top and then you flip it over and it will be on the bottom and the old beef will be on the top: that's my million-dollar idea, I tell her.

She says I was talking about cows in my sleep that night.

~

I don't remember, but it seems about right.

~

I am climbing the ladder to the top of the silo. I am drunk. I am stoned. I can fly.

I am crawling up under the overpass. I am throwing a beer bottle onto the interstate. We used to throw walnuts on the road while we were waiting for the bus. It was a game to see if we could get cars to run over them. This is the same.

I am starting to shit. I pull down my pants. I take a dump in the tall grass.

My friend is pissing a pentagon on a concrete pad. It is surrounded by silos. The car lights light it up. I am lying down in the middle. I am possessed by the devil. I cry in the car.

~

There was more, though.

~

Losses are not lacks but rather surplus discarded.

~

We switch modes to escape the current one. We sleep when we are tired of being awake or overwhelmed or bored or sad. While within the new mode, sleep, we are mostly unaware of our previous mode, exhaustion. We can have dreams in which we relive the horrors of the waking hours. We can have sleepless nights in which we can't completely switch to sleep. We can get some sort of break from the conscious mode and its troubles. A break that is mostly not remembered. We remember transitions to/from sleep. We remember dreams and nightmares. We almost remember. We know we had a dream, but it escapes us. Most of sleep is nothing at all. Our (conscious) self simply disappears, only to reappear later with varying degrees of disorientation. We piece together what must have happened while we slept. The train must have arrived at the station. I am in a hotel, not at home. My partner must have already gotten up.

~

At the old school, where the paint was peeling from the concrete block, we are suddenly herded in to the next room, the one without windows. Across the large concrete lot between us, a sort of courtyard, we can hear the sound of students yelling. At any time, they could breech the exterior wall.

Scared, we take sledgehammers to the block, carving doorways through a labyrinth of classrooms and storage closets. We can hear them in the building but still at a distance. I fumble with the CCTV connections, trying to get a view. Eventually, I abandon the effort and scramble down to the first floor. As we enter the giant gym, filled with all sorts of equipment and shelves to the roof, I realize that I am sprouting. In various places on my body, appendages that look like seedy asparagus are growing. I use these to swing through the gym, grabbing hold of the bottom of the trusses, from shelf to shelf. There are two of us that make it safely across the gym. Two more are stuck partway, and we go back for them. We meet some students from the other school and exchange stories. They explain that at some point there was an escape in a small airplane owned by a parent of one of the students.

We leave the school. There is a checkpoint where they are sorting those who are infected from those who aren't. But I don't tell them.

~

A mode can just be a byproduct. A mode can just be an accident.

~

I hear the radio muffled through the door. I try to continue my dream – thinking I will remember I am dreaming. I see blue-yellow bright shadow-tracers where the windows are when I close my eyes.

~

We enter into a mode, daily, in which we are unaware and unsure of why. We sleep, and we are not the only ones. Sleep is a mode, a plane of existence, that takes hold of us as much as we of it.

~

My whole body jolts awake. Every muscle contracted in a twitch.

The jolt is a translation, albeit an abrupt one. It carries the information from the dream to your body and zaps you in to a new waking state. It is an escape mechanism. You feel yourself falling. Somehow, your body screams mayday, mayday. The muscles contract. You avoid hitting the ground. Now, you are there in bed. Sweaty with heart racing. Safe?

Was that a sound here that jolted me awake? Is there something I need to investigate, or can I escape by sleeping? Which mode is calling – the dream or the waking? Surely, that is half the terror of the jolt.

~

There is a dead man in the outhouse. He is sprawled out, sitting on the bench, clothed, but stabbed in the chest. I see him every time I am about to open the door.

~

Dreams seep in to waking life and back. The borders are not so hard. I have trouble distinguishing between memory and dream, between waking and dreaming. Dreams influence how I feel about things. The houses I have lived in exist as dreams and memories intertwined. Our Chicago house exists at the end of a long walk by a river through the brick-sided apartment buildings and bungalows. Bricks, concrete, canal, cutting through. And up the stairs to a light-filled living room, open to the city and the trees and the cottonwood fluffs. Sometimes, I buy back that house. I return to find someone living in it. I beg and plead. The neighbors are still the same. Our children are still young.

~

It is only a reconstruction that we connect. Images and sounds and feelings and actions. Disjointed percepts. Ambivalent coming to.

~

Each gap becomes useful at the same time we deny our actual use of it. We claim sleep is for the mind to rewire itself, to rejuvenate, to aid the conscious moments. We deny our use of it as an escape from this world.

The memory, the dream, the imagination interact with one another. They speak in their different tongues.

Primary to their use is how they do not translate.

~

Constant whisper of the fan. The bare breasts. The turn. The blankets clutched. Pulled-up warmth. The back of the head. A rise and fall.

~

We attempt to translate. To bridge the gap, to span the modes. We produce again differently. We re-produce. We state that the identity is unchanged. A core remains. A continuity exists despite the new medium. I put my dreams in words. I put my words in dreams.

We do not translate. Things are lost. This is a strength of having many modes. Some do not conduct to the others. We get a break. There is too much. It is whittled down to a thin line we claim as a continuous life, a singular self. We ignore the vast overflows and losses. We use the vast overflows. This we will not translate. This we will translate loosely. This we will call a translation. I am the dream. I am the word. I am not.

~

Modes are incomplete in themselves. Modes include their own failures.[1]

~

I am at a church. There are other professors there. They are beseeching me to shave. I go back to the mirror in the hall. I have shaving cream all over my face. I start to shave. The long black straight whiskers do not want to come off. I return to the sanctuary partially shaven. I have shaving cream on my face. I occasionally try to make a pass with the razor.

~

We attempt to salvage, to cut the losses, to create a continuity. I was here all along, holding the washcloth. I was here all along, dreaming that dream. I was here all along, after the pinch. We tell ourselves a story of one life. We ignore the jolts, the absences, the abysses. Instead, we cast a line, drop breadcrumbs. We integrate the very things that are disintegrated.

~

Losses are just as much a part of the self/other/world as that which is translated.

~

Note

1 "It is inevitable that the Plan(e), thus conceived, will always fail, but that the failures will be an integral part of the plan(e). . . . So the plan(e) – life plan(e), writing plan(e), music plan(e) – must necessarily fail for it is impossible to be faithful to it; but the failures are a part of the plan(e) for the plan(e) expands or shrinks along with the dimensions of that which it deploys in each instance (planitude of n dimensions)." Deleuze and Guattari, *A Thousand Plateaus*, 269.

Bibliography

Deleuze, Gilles, and Félix Guattari. *A Thousand Plateaus: Capitalism and Schizophrenia*. Translated by Brian Massumi. Minneapolis, MN: University of Minnesota Press, 1987.

6 Embrace

~

I hear her talking on the teleconference. I hear the hum of the fridge. There are yellow beans in the field. The wind blows, showing the underside of the maple leaves on the trees. Her voice is muffled. I catch a word here and there. "Portfolios." "Supervisors." Her meeting overlaps in to my writing. It syncs up on these words. I try to ignore them. I try to embrace them. "Coordinator." "Family interview." The other voices, too, that poor sound quality like talking through a cardboard tube. I just let the words wash over me, more clear now. Our kitchen has a swarm of flies right now. I put up the flytape. There are a lot stuck there. Disgusting. "Yes, yes, yes." "No I don't." "Rubric." I relax in. I meditated this morning for 10 minutes. Ten minutes because they are supposed to be here to deliver the wood any minute. Its 10:30. They said 10. The cat meows. The dogs pounce. I hear the refrigerator again. I know it is there the whole time, but I lose it, and then it comes back. I've been writing 12 minutes. my goal is 30. I listen a few moments, giving up on persevering through writing. They just called. Beaver Tree. They are on their way with the wood.

~

This body is one too many.

This body hangs on me, heavy.

They assure me you cannot live without a body.

They assure me you can live forever without a body.

I'm not sure who to believe. Mainly, I just go on. Eating. Sleeping. Shitting.

~

Yesterday, they cut the green field. Suddenly, it was light with long stripes of a deep dark. When I went to bed, they were still out there with the tractors. Lights on rumbling.

This morning, the field was cleared. The bright light green faded to a brown.

The road runs next to the field. There are greens and blues. Browns. A mosaic of asphalt. My wandering attention creates a collage. Letters of

DOI: 10.4324/ 9781003471882-9

recommendation for student teachers. Asphalt. Grade reading reflections. Field. Rocks for the driveway getting delivered. Other people's driveways. Breath. Walk faster.

I can feel the wind filling in behind my arms as they swing forward. Rushing to fill in the low pressure. The beginning of flight.

~

Living is swimming in excess, breathing in the surplus. It's not a surplus at all but a great many that we are part of and that we have mistaken as other, as if only a small part is self.

~

Today, it is the birds and the windchimes and the refrigerator hum. People are distracted 47% of the time. Which part counts as distraction? Are those sounds the distraction to writing, or is it the other way around? Is it possible to hold it all at once? Or does attention just vacillate? We notice one small part now and another small part then. We can try to notice all the parts by calming the mind. The thinking, the distraction, also serves a purpose.

We jump from thing to thing, sometimes intentionally, sometimes not. We automatically see objects as three dimensional. We assume the side we cannot see. We greatly overestimate what we know. We fill in the unknown. We ignore the unknown.

~

There are gloved fingers in my mouth. I feel the latex on my tongue.

"Hey, little girl, is your daddy home? Did he go away and leave you all alone?"[1]

Is my tongue touching her fingers on purpose? I try not to think about it because I think that might be making it worse.

I bet they get some real creeps in here.

"Woa-oa-oa-ah. Audience: Woa-oa-oa-ah. Woa-oa-oa. Audience: Woa-oa-oa."

I try not to look at her face. I've practiced this. Looking in between the mask and the parabolic light. There is the grid of the fluorescent light cover. I focus on it. A grid of light and dark.

I don't know how people with children do it.

Do you have school-age children?

No, one on the way. Finding daycare was difficult enough.

"Then the rain let up and the sun came up. And we were gettin' dry."[2]

I feel her warm stomach against the top of my head. I feel warm toward her. Expecting. A mother.

Did you get pictures of that? You can see the hole here.

It looks solid to me.

I have time, I tell her. I look at those weird glasses, like two jeweler's scopes. I look away.

“And it stoa-oa-oa-oa-oaned me to my soa-oa-oal.”

I am sitting up now. It will take time. You’ll feel a pinch, she said.

A pinch.

“Sleight of hand and twist of fate.”[3]

I can tell someone has been planning this display. There is a string-art “smile” sign. A sticker that says Hygiene Proud Colgate. A little placard that says “like us on Facebook” with the Wi-Fi password: smile:):). All carefully arranged around the window directly in front of the chair, looking out on the parking lot.

I think it’s working, I’m feeling great.

I hear myself laughing at my own joke. I realize I am alone in the room.

I am inspecting the plastic cover of the fluorescent light.

You will feel a vibration.

Do you prefer a bite guard?

Raise your hand if you need to swallow.

Would you stay if she promised you heaven?

I raise my hand.

“Rhia-ia-ia-nen”[4]

They give me a sheet. My blood pressure is high. They took it five times. You should get it checked out.

~

We never start with nothing, with a blank canvas. It has already begun. Structures are already in place.

Living involves exhaling. Urinating. Defecating. Shedding skin and hair and nails.[5]

~

The flies keep landing on my head. I stop. I wave them away with my hand.

~

The buzzing of the fridge turns in to an oscillation turns in to a higher buzzing oscillation I suppress that there is more that falls back to silence or a quieter hum the sound of swallowing what I was going to say but.

~

There I am. There I was. There’s me. That’s me. There we are. There we were. This is there. Here we are. This is at. This is when.

~

I attempt to focus, to listen. Inevitably, my thoughts march through, carrying me off unaware of the buzz of the refrigerator or the singing of the wood stove. But those distractions, daydreams, are just as real. They are a different mode, a different type of real, but still just as real. It is this acceptance of the overloading of daily life, of the disjunctures and tangents, that allows us to claim all of our life – not just the parts for which we were “really present.”

I am disjointed. I use nonconductors. They use me. Here, I am carried off. Here, I try to be carried off. Here, I come to another mode, a listening. Here, I find myself in a another mode, a thinking. Here, I find myself also there. Here, I claim both the here and the there.

~

"There we are" shows our displacement from the present, our absence, and yet it also shows our doubling over – our ability to exist here and there, now and then simultaneously.[6] "There we are" is a hybrid – another time/place ("there") combined with this time/place ("are"). We exist in multiple times and places, in this moment and those past.

We overcome the idea of a singularly located self.

~

I keep turning over from side to side, occasionally on my belly or back. I can't get to sleep. I can't get comfortable. My stomach hurts. I could write about this. Did I take my sleep medicine? Yes. If I focus, I can ignore my son's TV sound coming through the hall, I can ignore my wife's breathing, I can suddenly hear the crickets over the sound of the cicadas. It's cool enough tonight we don't have the fan on. It reminds me of childhood, that sound. A sleepy sound. But then it is gone, and I hear the TV and the breathing and not the crickets and cicadas. I focus again. Relax but focus. Listen. There it is again. I am swimming away from the swimmers. They murdered my friends. I am trapped. I stab the swimmer about to attack me. I am not sure I did the right thing. I am turning over again. Focus on the cicadas, the night sounds. My stomach hurts. The other swimmers on my team seem jealous. I have been selected to hold one side of the large dark-red banners at the front. I am getting up to get my stomach medicine. We aren't swimming anymore but marching through the air. It is like a band performance. We are in an enormous stadium in the sky, there is no ground plane beneath us, just the stands filled with people all around, a wall of spectators surrounding an enormous playing area. We are hovering there. I am trying to learn the new moves with the banner. I get the dogs and let them out. I toast the bagels and slather cream cheese on them and set them on top of the lunches I made. I gave the wrong bagel to the wrong child. My wife switches them.

~

There are hard separations, cliffs. There are clouds and mists and endless blue skies. There are waters with currents. Spaces with more compression here and less there.

But there is surely not one smooth space.

~

All there is is the remnants of a dream and a bird singing. All there is is the remnants of a dream and a bird singing and a car passing. All there is is the remnants of a dream and a bird singing and a car passing and a muffled radio. All there is is a bird singing and a car passing and a muffled radio and footsteps on the stairs. All there is is footsteps on the stairs. All there is is a doorknob rattling and a door opening. All there is is syllables saying. All there is is what they mean.

~

We use nonunification of the senses, nonunification of the stories, nonunification of the reals. We exclude in order to focus. We relax in order to be surprised. We lie. We go back on our word. We love these complex nonunified worlds. We are escaping.

~

Consciousness is never 100%. I am always distracted, overloaded, sleepy, focused. The world goes on without me. My approximations are generally good enough. I try to catch up on what I missed. I hear enough to get me by most of the time. I fill in the blanks. Life is discontinuous, partial, halting. We play the probabilities. We brute force it. We work with rough dimensions and rules of thumb. The calculations are back of the envelope.

But when this becomes obvious, we circle the wagons. We declare continuity, comprehensiveness, certainty. Surely, we are not operating with such tentative and approximate beliefs. We project confidence, hoping to fool ourselves.

What would it mean to acknowledge this? To see life "as a pure many". To look at the "nonconductors" and how we use them?[7] To see our rough framing, our changing working truths, our sudden shifts. We can resettle our very idea of reality in a moment, marking it off as just a dream, just a thought, just a feeling. The walls and gates are ever ready to stop the flood, to change the moment, to cut a new real.

~

I also see it from outside myself, watching myself.

~

Notes

1 Springsteen, "I'm on Fire".
2 Morrison, "And It Stoned Me".
3 U2, "With or Without You".
4 Fleetwood Mac, "Rhiannon".
5 "But there's no trace of an 'I' in your body. Not one of your cells lives longer than ten years." Droit, *Astonish Yourself*, 7.
6 "Re-Membering Home Movies" in Tillett, *Living the Questions*.
7 James, *Pragmatism*, 68.

Bibliography

Droit, Roger-Pol. *Astonish Yourself: 101 Experiments in the Philosophy of Everyday Life*. New York: Penguin Publishing Group, 2003.

Fleetwood Mac. "Rhiannon", recorded February 1975, track 4 on Fleetwood Mac, Reprise Records, vinyl LP.

James, William. *Pragmatism & the Meaning of Truth*. Cambridge, MA: Harvard University Press, 1978.

Morrison, Van. "And It Stoned Me", recorded Summer 1969, track 1 on Moondance, Warner Brothers, vinyl LP.

Springsteen, Bruce. "I'm on Fire", recorded May 11, 1982, track 4 on Born in the U.S.A., Columbia, vinyl LP.

Tillett, Wade. *Living the Questions: Dispatches from a Life Already in Progress*. Charlotte, NC: Information Age Pub., 2017.

U2. "With or Without You", recorded 1986, track 3 on *The Joshua Tree*, Island, vinyl LP.

Part III

Multiplication of the Real

7 Hesitate

The waitress asks me if I am ready to order. I turn to my family. I ask them if they are ready. I decide. I'm not ready. We're not ready. Can you come back in a few minutes?

The waitress turns to leave.

I buy myself some time. I savor this moment. This moment – when I can have anything, everything. This moment before decision. This moment of decision. Now, here, I suspend myself now and here.

I ask my family what they are having.

I am pausing, recirculating, embracing the potential. We are all alive with decision. Time. I seek this opening as it opens. I seek this breaking as it breaks.

I'm trying to decide between corned beef hash or the patty melt.

Here, I live in multiple worlds. I draft hints. I draft hunches. I am the selves that I will be soon, branching. All of them. They are me and I am them.

I try to listen to my daughter.

. . . And then the pole vaulter threw his pole down and started charging at him.

I love the bliss of forgetting, of forgetting to decide, of knowing that I will decide anyway, Of pushing it down, down to a subconscious, of pushing it out of thought, of letting it brew. I feel it building even though I don't think it. Soon, I will decide, and yet, for now, I am deciding – without thought – without method – things are happening. I have faith.

After a while, the waitress comes again.

Are you ready to order now?

Oh crap, yes, I mean sure, come to me last, though.

The other family members order.

And for you?

Um, I guess I'll have . . .

I watch, from the outside, to see what my decision will be. That's the thing about choosing: You don't know what your choice is until you've made it. Before that, in the in-between, you have choices.

~

DOI: 10.4324/ 9781003471882-11

The gap haunts us and hunts us. But we are part of it. We use it against itself to create our selves.

We double it over and say, see, there is something here. There is a hesitation.[1]

We are bubbles of hesitation. We are gaps within the gaps. In between, we work frantically to rewire.

~

Hesitation does not just exist within us. It is fundamental to the world. It is indetermination. It is the ability to create the new.[2]

~

Is there a difference between perceiving and conceiving a gap? Do we perceive that we are forgetting, that we have forgotten, that we are asleep or were asleep? Or is it some sort of deduction, that the world must have gone on without us? Perception cannot be separated from its conception/deduction.

If perception perceives objects as possibilities-limits,[3] what are the possibilities-limits perceived of a gap? For space, there is the possibility of movement, a lack of objects impeding.

The gap can't be separated from its uses, from its possibility-limits, as that is exactly what a gap is (to us). To conjure up a certain sort of gap/mode is to conjure up its affordances.[4]

Modes, actions, objects, gaps can't be separated.

~

The Bobcat is here. It all seems backwards to me. Right foot is a pedal that works both toe and heel to tilt the bucket. That part makes sense. Left foot is a toe-heel pedal that moves the bucket up and down. Right arm moves the right side forward or back. Left arm moves the left side forward and back. Too many appendages to keep track of, to learn. I move gravel in the bucket. I put the bucket down, front edge angled to the ground. I push the bucket down until my front wheels are off the ground. I go backward. The rocks get scraped off the high points. The rocks fill in the low points.

I am learning a new body.

~

Hesitation is not where a pure perception is seen or pure affect is felt – there is no such thing. Hesitation is built into perception itself.

Feeling, memory, exist in the hesitation, as the hesitation. Our memories, feelings, are collectively constructed.[5] What I so often take to be my personal feelings and memories and thoughts are not only personally constructed.[6] Feelings are not "prior" to cognition or the social. They are not an immediate or transparent conduit to the real. The "internal" affects and memories and thoughts (as well as what counts as internal) are products of society.[7] So are the lack of affect and memories and thought. This can be from repression and suppression or from a "failure" to register. Blind spots are not only exploited but engineered and constructed.

Because there is hesitation, the gap, we can further process beyond what appears automatic; "automatic" itself being a mixture of memory, cognition, and senses. We can reconfigure. We can choose (to some degree).[8]

~

We are all only a few words from oblivion. We study those words so we will not say them. Trembling.

~

Decisions unfold. We slowly come to understand there is a decision, a fork. We inhabit doubt. We look at the forks. We make a decision, tentatively. The decision's implications begin to unfold. We doubt. We make modifications. We pause. We make a decision, tentatively. The decision unfolds. The decision is made. We doubt. The decision impacts other decisions. It cascades. It lives. It moves beyond the limits we thought it had. We inhabit this new real. Created beyond us.

~

A gap opens between birth and death, where the universe peeks at itself, where it hesitates.

~

I feel the tooth. Is it loosening? My tongue continues to touch it. It is loosening. I push it back and forth. I can feel underneath of it. Should I pull it? I keep working it back and forth. I can feel underneath of it. I test it with my fingers. Give it a small tug. Not ready. I push it around with my tongue. I give it a yank. The tooth remains. I consider tying it with a string to a doorknob. I heard that works. I grab it with my fingers. The tooth comes out.

~

The gap is consciousness. The interval between stimulus and response.[9]

~

The beat. The heartbeat.

~

We cascade into new states. We exist between dimensions. We operate in the precipice. We live in a critical state.[10]

~

We are the gap. We are synapses.[11] We are open problems, problematic fields.[12]

~

We are tubes and wires and cavities. Liquids and gases and electrical sparks. Interfaces within and without. Cascading to consciousness.

~

Adam and Eve were already screwed. Biting the apple wasn't the moment that gave them consciousness and banishment. It was the moment before. The pause. The contemplation. The temptation. Doubt with a forked tongue. This was the original sin: hesitation itself. Consciousness. To consider your own choice places you above God. That is a sin.

We are cast out, we are sinners, as soon as self-conscious thought occurs. What if I . . . The I is that hesitation, that moment beyond god, where we claim godlike status for ourselves. We imagine this could be other. We create this other. We are absent from our present by virtue of this hesitation, this self-consciousness, this doubt.

Paradise exists in banishment, in awareness, in nostalgia. We were born of Doubt with a forked tongue. We saw the forking paths. We realized we could choose. We hesitated a moment. We created ourselves.

~

Notes

1 "[T]he living being essentially has duration; it has duration precisely because it is continuously elaborating what is new and because there is no elaboration without searching, no searching without groping. Time is this very hesitation, or it is nothing." Bergson, *The Creative Mind*, 93.

2 "[T]ime is what hinders everything from being given at once. . . . Would not the existence of time prove that there is indetermination in things? Would not time be that indetermination itself?" Bergson, *The Creative Mind*, 93.

3 "Then, our conception of these effects is the whole of our conception of the object." Peirce, *Philosophical Writings*, 31.

4 "The objects which surround my body reflect its possible action upon them." Bergson, *Matter and Memory*, 7.

5 "Memory is collectively configured." Cole summarized in Middleton and Brown, *Experience*, 26.

6 "For the affect is not a personal feeling, nor is it a characteristic; it is the effectuation of a power of the pack that throws the self into upheaval and makes it reel." Deleuze and Guattari, *A Thousand Plateaus*, 240.

7 "The soul is the effect and instrument of a political anatomy; the soul is the prison of the body." Foucault, *Discipline and Punish*, 30.

8 Affect is felt in this interval; feeling is also remembering – including habits/perceptions. Al-Saji, "A Phenomenology of Hesitation", 143. Hesitation means the chance to change our affects, our responses, our perceptions. Al-Saji, "A Phenomenology of Hesitation", 144.

9 "[T]he consciousness of a living being may be defined as an arithmetical difference between potential and real activity. It measures the interval between representation and action." Bergson, *Creative Evolution*, 145.

10 "Rodent brains showed all the hallmarks of moving through a critical state as they cycled between sleep and wakefulness." Ouellette, "Rat Brains."

11 "If the mental objects of philosophy, art, and science (that is to say, vital ideas) have a place, it will be in the deepest of the synaptic fissures, in the hiatuses, intervals, and meantimes of a nonobjectifiable brain, in a place where to go in search of them will be to create." Deleuze and Guattari, *What Is Philosophy?*, 209.

12 "Being (what Plato calls the Idea) 'corresponds' to the essence of the problem or the question as such. It is as though there were an 'opening,' a 'gap,' an ontological 'fold' which relates being and the question to one another. In this relation, being is difference itself." Deleuze, *Difference and Repetition*, 64.

Bibliography

Al-Saji, Alia. "A Phenomenology of Hesitation: Interrupting Racializing Habits of Seeing." In *Living Alterities: Phenomenology, Embodiment, and Race*, edited by Emily Lee, 133–172. Albany: State University of New York Press, 2014.

Bergson, Henri. *The Creative Mind: An Introduction to Metaphysics*. New York: Wisdom Library, 1946.

———. *Creative Evolution*. Translated by Arthur Mitchell. Mineola, NY: Dover, 1998.

———. *Matter and Memory*. Translated by Nancy Margaret Paul and W. Scott Palmer. Dover Philosophical Classics. Mineola, NY: Dover Publications, 2004.

Deleuze, Gilles. *Difference and Repetition*. Translated by Paul Patton. New York: Columbia University Press, 1994.

Deleuze, Gilles, and Félix Guattari. *A Thousand Plateaus: Capitalism and Schizophrenia*. Translated by Brian Massumi. Minneapolis, MN: University of Minnesota Press, 1987.

———. *What Is Philosophy?* New York: Columbia University Press, 1994.

Foucault, Michel. *Discipline and Punish: The Birth of the Prison*. Translated by A Sheridan. 2nd Vintage Books ed. New York: Vintage Books, 1995.

Middleton, David, and Steve D. Brown. *The Social Psychology of Experience: Studies in Remembering and Forgetting*. London: Sage, 2005.

Ouellette, Jennifer. "Rat Brains Provide Even More Evidence Our Brains Operate Near Tipping Point." *Ars Technica*, June 7, 2019. https://arstechnica.com/science/2019/06/does-the-human-brain-teeter-on-the-edge-of-chaos-rat-brains-point-to-yes/.

Peirce, Charles Sanders. *Philosophical Writings of Peirce*. Edited by Justus Buchler. New York: Dover, 1955.

8 Doubt

~

I am terrified to think that you have secrets. That I have secrets. Even from myself. That we are complex and unknowable beings. That shadows haunt our every glance. That these stories are not much more than a light snow, melting under the slightest touch of light. That "I'm sorry" can't even begin to cover what we don't even know we could be sorry for. I tried to be me. I tried to be you. I am left with . . .

~

No, I can't even say "I am" . . . for both words allege too much. Too much unity.[1] Here, there were movements, navigations. Here, there were configurations, confluences, divergences. Here. There. There. Here.

~

This could be other. Things are not as they seem. I am grabbing only what I want to see. The truth will come out. You will see that I have only shown what I wanted to be seen. And I will see that. About you. About me.

~

Don't.

~

That's what I wish I said. But what I said was, there are no guarantees. But you have to try, right?

How lame.

~

I want to be loved. I am terrified to be loved. I trust you. I do not trust you.

~

Joseph woke in a cold sweat. The angel of Doubt blazing forward. Joseph was blinded by a realization. I will raise the child as my own.

The umbilical cords stretch all the way back, from mother to mother. The unknowable stretches all the way back, from father to father. Who was my

DOI: 10.4324/ 9781003471882-12

father? Doubt is there, ready to reveal itself. So many secrets carried to the grave. Am I the father?

~

God was a deadbeat dad. He created a son and abandoned him down here. Just like he did to us.

~

My son bound and gagged before me. Firstborn. I have heard the Lord. I am a true believer. I raise the crooked knife. I do not hear the Lord. In the thicket, something rustles. It is Doubt, fully formed with horns. It must have been lurking there, beneath God, before God. A power to decide to believe, the crooked knife raised. And yet, belief fails. In the critical moment, the foundation is exposed, undermined.

~

Our attention turns to the thicket. We raise the knife. We attempt to sacrifice Doubt itself. But the hesitation already occurred. The hesitation always already occurs. Doubt is the condition from which we arise, from which consciousness was handed down.

We pray. We commune. We sacrifice. It only reinforces our separation. Cemented. Buried. We try to kill Doubt.

~

Doubt is a whole other world. I oscillate between them. Here, it all makes sense. Over here, it also all makes sense. I repurpose the facts. I remake the truths. I operate with two worlds, never knowing which I will wake to.

I train. I analyze. I look at the possibilities and limits of the two worlds. I choose one I can live with. I practice belief. I usher away the other world, the doubt. It continues to exist, fully formed, right through the doorway.

I exist between the son and the ram, the table and the thicket. Both branches have been taken. I took the knife to doubt. It only multiplied.

~

Three days between death and resurrection.

~

There is a difference in desire, in timing. The other is unknowable. We wish to overcome this, to align desires, to format the other to match. We wish to believe.

~

Let me.

~

That is where one can wedge yourself in, take advantage, leverage doubt. This is the secret of the secret. This is the lie of the lie. Beyond all certainty, underneath it, like a muddy riverbed. It is the unanswerability of that most human of horrors: What if? What if it was always there, just under the surface? What if I read it wrong? What if this was so shiny just to distract me? What if I've been wrong all along? What if . . .

And I want to say yes, but this time, I've found it. Yes, but this time, I've bored down to the truth. Bedrock.

But its muck all the way down. It isn't a what if on top of what if but rather the undercurrent where muck and river meet. The backside of what if. The fact that it doesn't all add up, no matter how you add it. We think it is only fractures in a whole. It is all muck and quicksand. The doubt doesn't come from partial truth. The truth itself is nowhere to be found.[2] Doubt is the least of our problems. The problem is the facts we are doubting. We hold on to their promise, scared that is all they have to give. Through doubt, we placed ourselves above truth. Truth is sucked dry, an empty skin. We dare to ask what if. The world crumbles from there.

~

Please.

~

Notes

1 "Over and over, the ego must solve the problem of love. What belongs to the ego, and what belongs to the object? Is it me, or is it them? How do I know that what I think is happening is actually happening?" Britzman, *Lost Subject, Contested Objects*, 12.

2 "[S]ince we are inside truth and cannot get outside it, all that I can do is define a truth within the situation." Merleau-Ponty quoted by Prigogine and Stengers, *Order Out of Chaos*, 299.

Bibliography

Britzman, Deborah P. *Lost Subjects, Contested Objects: Toward a Psychoanalytic Inquiry of Learning*. Albany: State University of New York Press, 1998.

Prigogine, Ilya, and Isabelle Stengers. *Order Out of Chaos: Man's New Dialogue with Nature*. London: Heinemann, 1984.

9 Divide

~

Excuses are just fictions anyway.

That's what she said. She didn't mean it.

Wiping away the cover, unveiling the tracks that she worked and didn't work to conceal.

You can't take that from me, in one glancing swoop.

I want to appear whole. I will see the reflected glimmer. Unwhole me. Camouflage. You. Me – restored radiant shining back.

And those, those sound like just mechanics. But they are transformations.

~

I'm sure you haven't been fooled by my pretenses to honesty. I have.

I refuse to tell. I have secrets. I jump over them as if they are not there. Not just to you, but to me. Writing isn't just about projecting a self but about (re)constructing selves. It is always selves – discontinuous. A blind eye. An "ignore-ance".[1]

I refuse to tell my deepest struggles, my worst transgressions, my excuses. For fear you will hate me. I will hate myself. You will blame me. You will not understand. The gap between you and me is really not something we can bridge.

These stories are full of holes, through and through. Spaces between words and letters, and even within the e's and the o's and others. Tiny holes everywhere. A million black holes, a space foam.[2] Electrons and photons, the ambiguity of the wave and the particle contains within it a refusal. Forces repel, refusing to touch. We float on empty spaces. We are spaces.

I want to love myself, have a self, stand for something. I have a blind eye. I use it to full effect. How else can change occur? I must betray myself.[3]

There is nothing to forgive here. Move along.

~

DOI: 10.4324/ 9781003471882-13

I will never tell you my true regrets. And if I did, I would intersperse them with fiction. The unreliable narrator is a shield.

I have no regrets.

~

Freedom comes in hypocrisy. The divided self is leveraged in different directions. I pursue contradictory, appealing paths. I work against my integration, my unification. Refusal claims freedom, diversity, options to take up different modes in different contexts and situations. The "true self" is not only overvalued, it is a fiction we actively work against – with varying degrees of consciousness of that fact. Oh, Lord, unify me but not yet.[4]

~

Redemption leaps the gap, creating sudden discontinuities. The past self is dislodged. The past actions are discharged. There is a new birth, disjointed.

~

Regrets crawl out of a hole. I could have been other. I could have acted other. I repent. I will be other. I will act other.

I always find myself on the outside of redemption.

I will keep my secrets.

~

There are only redemptions, never singular or permanent. The best we can hope for is those moments, these moments, when we embrace the spaces.

~

It's not just about the strength of belief, but also, can I live with the consequences of certain beliefs?

And sometimes, I end up just in a suspension of belief but living a truth based on those consequences.

Truth without belief. Operational truth. Instrumental truth.[5]

~

I have a battery of truths. I deploy them selectively, as the situation allows.[6]

~

We inhabit doubt. We carry within us both truths, innumerable truths. We suspend belief, true belief, and work with an operational belief. We consider the consequences, the possibilities, the limits, the selves, the worlds that we can engage with through this truth AND that one. These truths contradict, split apart. We can force a selection. We can choose a truth singular. Or we can wait. We hold them both. We attempt to keep them from touching, from destroying one another. We walk in to one world. We wake into another.

It is easy to dis-integrate. We do it all the time.

~

It isn't easy to dis-integrate. Things become pressing, important. Things become obsessive and unescapable. I feel my self splitting in two. This is not comfortable. Worlds impinge on me, begging, demanding. This is the truth, they say. I can't live with that. Or that.

I feel rather unprepared. The expectation always seems to integrate, to solidify, to find a singular. Even if we have always blinded ourselves to our own role in the construction and exceptions to these singulars. We write a Truth while living through truths.

But dare I make the Truth into truths?

This goes against an inner nature, a social expectation, a conception of self and world. It could very well be the death of me.

~

If Abraham gave his son, we would be aligned, inhabiting, with only our personal conversation instead of ethics.[7]

Sacrifice is accomplished by a betrayal. God gave his son.

Eloi. Eloi. Why have you forsaken me?

A New Testament. Living in the Holy Spirit. Inhabiting the fire. Talking in tongues.

The economy is broken by a betrayal, a turning away. Cutting out the poison. A whole is made.

There is a continual turning away, a continual death and rebirth. Exorcising. Salvation is in the saving, in the act of moving on, of refusing consistency, of accepting new growth and pruning the old.

As if I could abide by such betrayal.

As if I could escape it.

~

It cannot be repaid. We are in too deep, too long, too many missed ticking beats. I should just forgive and forget. "I only live once" and other clichés soothe me but not really.

~

I'm sorry.

~

Notes

1 Felman cited in Ellsworth, *Teaching Positions*, 55.
2 Minsky, "Universe Bubbles."
3 Jagodzinski and Wallin, *Arts-Based Research*.
4 St. Augustine: "For I was afraid thou wouldst hear me too soon, and heal me at once of my disease of lust, which I wished to satiate rather than see extinguished." James, *Religious Experience*, 172.
5 James, *Pragmatism*, 98.

6 "Any idea upon which we can ride, so to speak; any idea that will carry us prosperously from any one part of our experience to any other part, linking things satisfactorily, working securely, simplifying, saving labor; is true just so much, true in so far forth, true *instrumentally*." James, *Pragmatism*, 34.
7 Kierkegaard, *Fear and Trembling*.

Bibliography

Ellsworth, Elizabeth Ann. *Teaching Positions: Difference, Pedagogy, and the Power of Address*. New York: Teachers College Press, 1997. http://smudgestudio.org/archive/writing/Teaching%20Positions%20EE.pdf.

Jagodzinski, Jan, and Jason Wallin. *Arts-Based Research: A Critique and a Proposal*. Boston: Brill, 2013. https://brill.com/view/title/36660.

James, William. *Pragmatism & the Meaning of Truth*. Cambridge, MA: Harvard University Press, 1978.

———. *The Varieties of Religious Experience: A Study in Human Nature: Being the Gifford Lectures on Natural Religion Delivered at Edinburgh in 1901–1902*. Mineola, NY: Dover Publications, 2002.

Kierkegaard, Søren. *Fear and Trembling*. Translated by W. Lowrie. Princeton, NJ: Princeton University Press, 1974.

Minsky, Carly. "The Universe Is Made of Tiny Bubbles Containing Mini-Universes, Scientists Say." *Vice* (blog), October 24, 2019. www.vice.com/en_us/article/j5yngp/the-universe-is-made-of-tiny-bubbles-containing-mini-universes-scientists-say.

10 Make

~

I know this coffee cup is real. I can tell from the flaws and imperfections. The glazing doesn't quite reach the bottom. The lip is too thick. The circle, which looks circular to me, would never live up to snuff in the mind of Plato. What exists here has fallen from grace. A shoddy replica. A sin.

I ask for forgiveness. I am never made whole. Redemption only truly comes in death. When I will see the true circle.

I can't help it, I cherish these secondhand objects. Their failures only make them more vivid, alive. They change and chip and anger God again and again. I imagine the heavenly blank white walls where each blemish would stand out even more.[1] Smudges in the radiance. I'm going to bring this cup with me as a reminder. A stowaway.

~

Hesitation can work both ways, as the gap between the experience and thought as the "real," or the gap between experience and action as "thought." While these separations cannot be pure, that is not to say they are without use. When we open ourselves and listen beyond the object/label, we find an excess of sensations that we constantly sort through and ignore as we focus.[2] We will never be able to escape all of our expectations and ignorances. Objects and labels are tentative and convenient tools (truths).[3] We both accept them and undermine them. We look at how they are constructed. We look at what they exclude.

~

There is not a direct line between experience and the real. There is no pre-cognitive, transparent perception of real uninterpreted stimuli.[4] We become predisposed to listen for certain things (syllables, for example), to see certain things (objects), to value or discard certain things (dreams). Perception is a mode of affixing concepts to sensory input to produce a reality. We are always involved in the recreation of the real. It doubles back on ourselves as experience.

~

DOI: 10.4324/ 9781003471882-14

The brain doesn't take in everything and select what is needed. It actively excludes in order to obtain some kind of focus. Many parts of reality never actually enter into the brain. Multiple reals exist. Perception is not a selection but rather an exclusion. A pairing with particular stimuli while ignoring anything else. Occasionally, the brain widens its perception to see if the exclusions should remain.[5] By gapping possible inputs (and note that these inputs themselves are supremely limited), a perception emerges – and from that, a world, a moment, a real. Neither past nor present exists purely for us.

~

The lights are dim. There is a low murmuring voice. Singing. Confessions. Burrowing to a truth, a failure. I give it over. I let God take it from me. To pray is to pray for God's will. To accept and be relieved.

It is so contrived. I think later. Mind control techniques. I am confident, critical. I realize too late I have cast myself out. Purged. Ostracized. Banished. Expelled.

I hold the stone in my pocket. Rounded with a ridge my thumb naturally runs along. I cling to this. This here now rock solid that presses back against my pressing. I cannot make it go away. I can be distracted. This remains in my hand, weighty. I rest in continuity, permanence, amidst the discontinuous. This is my escape from my thoughts, my alternative reals, my forking paths. In my hand, focus. This is with me, more real than me. An assurance. Insurance. Against the rampaging possibles disabling.

And finally the drugs helped too.

~

How does the real become real?[6] We are all already in a constant state of practice of opening or closing what counts as real. What we actually experience shifts as what counts as the real shifts and vice-versa. We have been learning this through our particular cultures and situations (also both changing) since birth. Long before birth, we evolved to detect certain wavelengths and to interpret them.

~

I am redeemed. The Spirit has come to reside in me. My desires are its desires.

And there above me, I reach out and grab the golden sword.[7] You wouldn't understand. This is a suspension, a direct connection, a portal. There is no inside and outside. God speaks to me. Here. There. Here is there. This is not ambiguous. This is not pretend. This is where the borders of the real drop away, passing through clouds.

I pray. I practice. The world turns itself inside out. Meaning blooms from the sidewalk, the cheese grater, the sugar cube. These are not mere replicas. They were placed here by God. As was I. I inhabit this, this mystical existence.

Sometimes, I fall out. I feel as if the Spirit has left me.

I pray. I practice.[8] My neighbor said unto me, Can you give me a ride to the grocery store? Thus the Lord spoke.

I am born once again.
I live a life ordained.[9]

~

With eddies and flows. I float in the doubts. Sometimes, I admit, this chair is just a chair. I feel myself becoming estranged. I pray. I practice.

~

I walk the paths. There are no paths to be seen, but there are my circuits slowly built up out of habit. The points where I pause. The vistas. A sip from the flask. To mark this place in time, to swallow it in. I am alive. I feel the burning in my throat. This sunlight, this air, this ground beneath my feet. Snowflakes like a snow globe. This is really happening.[10] I grasp. I am grasping. And between those two sentences lies the world.

~

It isn't 100%.[11] It is more like a suspension. We no longer call things imaginary. We no longer call things pretend.[12] It is a loosening of the borders of the real, of its rules.[13] We work to change the definitions.[14] We work past the old standard of what is real. When we are becoming the wolf, part of us is still not-wolf. We never arrive.[15] There is still doubt. The woman who talks with God, she doubts. She doubts and she continues.

I feel like I've ventured too far and not far enough.

I have the panic it is all too much, and yet nothing comes out, except this dribble, this slow text, letter by letter.

~

I am adjacent. I never really become the wolf. The sword never becomes real to me. I act it, but I know it is pretend.

People have conversations with God. It isn't 100%. Instead, it is a loosening of the borders of the real. It is a reorganization of real and imaginary, of self and other. It is an opening to the small daily wonders. But also an invention.

There is still doubt. You will be disappointed if you hang on to the old standard of what is real.

It is a becoming, not an arriving.

You are always already becoming.

~

Notes

1 Tillett, "Objectification."
2 Sartre called this foregrounding intentionality. Sartre, *Being and Nothingness*.
3 "We invent the truth to utilize reality, as we create mechanical devices to utilize the forces of nature. It seems to me one could sum up all that is essential in the pragmatic conception of truth in a formula such as this: *while for other doctrines a new truth is a discovery, for pragmatism it is an invention*." Bergson, *The Creative Mind*, 215.

4 "We can never really separate our mind from what it perceives." Davidson, "Healthy Minds App." "Insight and Why It Matters." "We assert, at the outset, that if there be memory, that is, the survival of past images, these images must constantly mingle with our perception of the present, and may even take its place." Bergson, *Matter and Memory*, 70.
5 Cepelewicz, "Brain Filters."
6 The question isn't just how God becomes real (Luhrmann). The bigger question is how the real becomes real. As Luhrmann states, those who practice experience different phenomenal events (immediate experience) from before. Luhrmann, *How God Becomes Real*. Latour looked at this from a scientific-rational viewpoint. Latour, *Never Been Modern*. Deleuze and Guattari also ask how the self becomes real, "to examine how subjectivity comes to be created and sustained . . . [and] how . . . to create different kinds of subjectivity." Koczy, *Beckett, Deleuze and Performance*, 76.
7 Tillett, "Living Hymns and Iterations," 1532.
8 Prayer practice changes perception. Luhrmann, *How God Becomes Real*.
9 See the "knight of faith." Kierkegaard, *Fear and Trembling*.
10 "Notice the label. And then break it down." Cortland Dahl in Davidson, "Healthy Minds App." "Insight: Beyond the Labels: Tip."
11 "We fall into a false alternative if we say that you either imitate or you are. What is the real is the becoming itself." Deleuze and Guattari, *A Thousand Plateaus*, 238.
12 Luhrmann explains that it begins as pretend, that we enter a space of play, where the normal rules are suspended. God becomes real when we move adjacent, suspend boundaries, pretend, and enter a state of play. Luhrmann, *How God Becomes Real*. In play, the rules are malleable – part of the game is changing the game.
13 "Starting from the forms one has, the subject one has, or the functions one fulfills, becoming is to extract particles between which one establishes the relations of movement and rest, speed and slowness that are closest to what one is becoming and through which one becomes. This is the sense in which becoming is the process of desire." Deleuze and Guattari, *A Thousand Plateaus*, 272.
14 "We also acknowledge that She is, in part, a product of our imaginations when we declare that we can remember and re-create ancient rites, 'Or, failing that, invent.'" Wise, *Hidden Circles*, 129.
15 "You have to keep enough of the organism for it to reform each dawn." Deleuze and Guattari, *A Thousand Plateaus*, 160.

Bibliography

Bergson, Henri. *The Creative Mind: An Introduction to Metaphysics*. New York: Wisdom Library, 1946.

———. *Matter and Memory*. Translated by Nancy Margaret Paul and W. Scott Palmer. Dover Philosophical Classics. Mineola, NY: Dover Publications, 2004.

Cepelewicz, Jordana. "To Pay Attention, the Brain Uses Filters, Not a Spotlight." *Quanta Magazine*, September 24, 2019. www.quantamagazine.org/to-pay-attention-the-brain-uses-filters-not-a-spotlight-20190924/.

Davidson, Richard. "Healthy Minds App." n.d. https://hminnovations.org/.

Deleuze, Gilles, and Félix Guattari. *A Thousand Plateaus: Capitalism and Schizophrenia*. Translated by Brian Massumi. Minneapolis, MN: University of Minnesota Press, 1987.

Kierkegaard, Søren. *Fear and Trembling*. Translated by W. Lowrie. Princeton, NJ: Princeton University Press, 1974.

Koczy, Daniel. *Beckett, Deleuze and Performance: A Thousand Failures and a Thousand Inventions*. New York: Springer, 2018.

Latour, Bruno. *We Have Never Been Modern*. Translated by C. Porter. Cambridge, MA: Harvard University Press, 1993.

Luhrmann, T. M. *How God Becomes Real: Kindling the Presence of Invisible Others*. Princeton, NJ: Princeton University Press, 2020. https://doi.org/10.1515/9780691211985.

Sartre, Jean-Paul. *Being and Nothingness*. Avenel, NJ: Gramercy Books, 1994.

Tillett, Wade. “Objectification.” 1998. http://cardinalscholar.bsu.edu/handle/handle/182927.

———. “Living Hymns and Iterations.” *Qualitative Inquiry* 14, no. 8 (December 1, 2008): 1526–1539. https://doi.org/10.1177/1077800408318422.

Wise, Constance. *Hidden Circles in the Web: Feminist Wicca, Occult Knowledge, and Process Thought*. The Pagan Studies Series. Lanham, MD: AltaMira Press, 2008.

11 Double

We swim down here at the bottom. Bottom dwellers, bottom feeders. Even the birds only briefly rise, and then it is not so high. An upward swoop only to be carried down. They pull up the worms, dive into the water. They gather force to penetrate the surface, ever so slightly. Mostly, we live on the ground plane. Our feet, our wheels are designed to float us here.

The ground plane advances on us. The years of dust and dirt, discarded human skin and hair, plant matter dried and crushed. The sidewalk gets lower every year. The soil and grass build up on its sides. Creeping, burying. We try to stay moving, stay floating. The soil will cover us.

Everything is fallen to this earth. We walk among the dirt and the air. It moves through us. Reconfigured matter. Oxygen to carbon dioxide. The atmosphere is blank and empty, offering little resistance. The wind reminds us. The sudden realization of the rise and fall of the breath. Air is our medium. We forget. The birds are the only real swimmers. We plod and crawl along.

There have been satellites and space stations. Hovering a little higher over the earth, refusing to crash because of their speed. And airplanes and airships and paragliders. But our real home is on the earth. The food and water and the vehicle itself are all built and prepared here, with roots digging in to an overturned crust.

Our wandering is mostly horizontal. We hardly dig or jump. We breathe one medium and walk on another. This border is where we live, floating and breathing. Until we are churned under. Ancient molecules reconfigured.

~

Architects plan time to plan space. The contractors sign a contract. They must place this brick here, within this time period, per the drawing and the agreement. To waver from that contract, if for instance, the contractor discovers a problem or proposes an improvement, a change order must be signed. The future actions must be in writing. There will be a charge. One way or the other, the balance is adjusted.

If, as an architect, I show up at the site and say, now that I see it, this would be so much better if . . . that is too bad, too late. It means a failure of previous imagination on my part.

DOI: 10.4324/ 9781003471882-15

Future space is contracted through future labor time. Movement through the space is anticipated, directed. Future pathways are delimited with walls built first with pixels and sealed with a pen.[1]

~

This house has the old glass. Curves in the telephone poles. Uneven velocities in the fields and tree branches. I pulled back all the drapes. The kids don't like that. People can see in. Especially at night. They tell them, I saw you in your house last night. They don't know that this house has the old glass.

~

I could be there, you know. A few steps away. Where the perspective is changed. I can imagine it now, what I look like here from there.

The screen split spits it back to me. My own image of me, here, talking, there, to you. It is from my point of view. It is from yours. It is me looking back at myself. It is you looking at me. Mostly, it is me looking at you looking at me. I flatter myself thinking that.

Sometimes, there is a glitch, and I hear my words coming back to me to, delayed. That was me a second ago. That was you receiving me just a half second ago. Space exists.

~

There is where I want to be. Back in the woods. Immune from email. Separated by distance, by the firewall of the two-track.

Here, I inhabit the there. I am there. I walk the woods. I pause at the ponds. I squat at the river. I take a sip.

Here, I write about it on my laptop. I am both places at once.

There, I inhabit the Here. That is what I tell myself. Even though I go out to download the email, the news, the texts. Even though I pull the cord on the generator, fire up the booster, start the hotspot.

~

We are both here and there.

~

Space is the illusion I operate daily with, that there is some sort of grid, empty places, where I could be, where I am not, where I am choosing not to be. I want to preserve my full agency and possibilities. It could have been different, right now. I could have been there instead of here. It can be different then. I could be there instead of here. I occupy it all at once. The places where I am not but could be are mine.

~

I made a lot of mistakes along the way. I rejected too many privileges. I accepted too many privileges. I never got what I deserve. I got more than I deserve.

I could have been an artist. I could have been a monk. I could have . . . I could have . . .

I could have been other. I have more potential. I am bigger than I am. My reality is but a small subset of the realities I inhabit in daydreams, nostalgia, and regret.

These exist as other places where I am possible. Lost possibles.

~

Where I am now means so much more because of where I could have been. Foreground against background. And even when I focus on the negative space, when I draw it in, I am left with the ghost of presence. A hole where an object is.

~

Despite all the stops and starts, there is something there in between. I existed. Somewhere between where I didn't and I won't.

There is a rhythm, like a Morse code. Combined, the rests and beats create a message, a music. Music doesn't mean something. It is lived. It exists. And then it is over, and it is as if it didn't.

When people write transcripts, sometimes, they write how long the pauses are. It would be interesting if I could capture how long the pauses are between these sentences, these thoughts. A silent brain humming away at something unknown, suddenly lurching forward in a direction. There are periods and paragraph breaks. They are not reliable indicators of the process. I sit here, watching the cursor blinking. Blinks between words, sentences. Blinks between birth, death.

I lose track of time all the time. Blinks and rests. Waking up when I didn't know I went to sleep. Time is a series of tunnels. We pop up from this rabbit hole or that one. Opening into different worlds, modes, memories.

~

Walking proceeds by gaps between feet. Displacements. We step over things. We put distance between each point planted. To follow a trail is to read both the spaces and the imprints.[2]

~

There was night. Now there is day. I was like that then. Someday, I will walk with a cane. The grandfathers prefer to use walking sticks. I walk with a walking stick. Sometimes. There are moments that aren't this one. I was then. I will be then.

I cast lines back between. The umbilical cords stretch back, tying us from womb to womb. I was then. I carry that with me. Within my womb. I will be then. I double back on myself. I am now and then, then and now.

I can dial up any of the times. Remaking now.

Until I can't.

Continuity of self comes from that discontinuity, from the ability to reach back and pull forward. To, out of thin air, conjure the self as a self-same self, a continuity. To claim, to acknowledge the abyss I just bridged. I am me now, only better. I was me then, only better. In between is a rounding of the clock, not the jumpy ticks of the second hand but the smooth motion of hours.

I double back. That is my self.

~

Notes

1 See "The Plan Abandoned" in Tillett, *Living the Questions.*

2 "Of course the walker proceeds by plantigrade steps, impressing on the ground a sequence of discrete footprints rather than a continuous trail. The storyteller does much the same, as John Berger has emphasized. 'No story,' he writes, 'Is like a wheeled vehicle whose contact with the road is continuous. Stories walk, like animals and men. And their steps are not only between narrated events but between each sentence, sometimes each word. Every step is a stride over something not said.'" Ingold, *Lines*, 95.

Bibliography

Ingold, Tim. *Lines: A Brief History*. London: Routledge, 2016.

Tillett, Wade. *Living the Questions: Dispatches from a Life Already in Progress*. Charlotte, NC: Information Age Pub., 2017.

Part IV

Claiming the Lack

12 Desire

~

I desire myself through her. I am loved. I am wanted. I am desired.[1]

I desire her. I desire her to desire me. She desires at different times, in different ways, for different things. A chasm opens. It is Yearning. A long-standing, deep-seated desire for something that is not – a whole alignment of the world, for desire to crackle through every moment, every word, every action.

~

I try not to see desire as lack. I experience lack.

~

Christianity is the creation of lack, the absence of God, the realization of the forgotten, the past's absence. Fundamental to remembering is the tearing apart from the present – a forgetting, a separation.[2]

~

I'm drinking until I collapse away from my desire, my drive. Usually, that's when I can't think, can barely walk, can mostly forget. I'm not trying to feel justified. I'm just taking it night by night.

~

We shouldn't suppose that desire exists first. Desire is not immune from social construction. Desire cannot be accessed "purely." Desire does not exist as some sort of primordial, natural drive that is then corrupted or steered. Desire is always already corrupted, steered, manipulated. Desire is shared. Desire is built.

The supposedly natural basis of desire is a prime means by which it is utilized. We both create desire and deny that it is a creation.[3] Instead, despite constructing an environment where the phenomenon will arise, the phenomenon is said to be discovered. Here, look, we have found your true desire. A part of your True Self™, of course. Let us help you become more of who you are . . .

~

DOI: 10.4324/ 9781003471882-17

To desire is to endlessly circle around the object[4] – not to fulfill desire but to inhabit desire. Lack is a sort of strange attractor, a planet around which we orbit. Lack becomes not lack. Lack becomes the plane of desire. Lack dissolves itself. The engine becomes a million tiny engines. For long moments, we forget we are in orbit. We are in a terrain, a space of forces and currents. Intensities.[5] Ebb and flow.

Lack becomes the gravitational pull. We are within the borders of the object of desire, within its influence, within its cloud. Electrons and space and attraction and velocity. Increasing towards a center?

Sometimes.

Further out, lack revolves around a complete object. It is solid. Other. Outside of reach. The fact that it still propels us indicates we are not completely outside of its influence, its forces.

Depending on the approach, lack can increase or encompass. Desire intensifies differently. Lack is the beginning of the inhabitation of desire. Or not.

Desire uses lack. Desire propels us forward. We are aligned. We shoot off in tangents. We settle into an orbit. We cascade to the center.

Desire perpetuates itself. Even the object reached is a wormhole. Things are turned inside out. Once again, we find ourselves approaching, within its reach, perpetuating as so many drones – controlled bodies.

~

I enter desire. I navigate forces and intensities. I inhabit a field. The borders of the self fall away. I am action. I move in light and shadow.

There is no lack, no missing object, no ultimate goal. There are currents and winds.

We set sail. We slow down. We build. We ride this moment, this feeling, this desire. We feel it take us in unanticipated ways. We surprise ourselves. This is the opening of an incomplete body, a partial self, embracing the cool breeze. We float downriver, seeing what is around the next curve, occasionally paddling around a downed tree.

This is my body, opened for you.

~

We are here now only until something better, until we are snatched away, raptured. Space and time are blinks of an eye in the face of eternity, and yet those blinks determine the infinite course. This world is terrible. I claim an infinite space beyond this one. Without death or misery or doubt. Infinite time to inhabit infinite space. My body, perhaps, will disperse so that I can inhabit it all as a medium. Energy fields.

There will be thought without doubt. The tree of knowledge will be extracted. We will sit content, basking in penetrating rays.

Time is a countdown. To death. To the apocalypse. To the leaving of this imperfect and limited world for a perfect and limitless one. This is hope. The future paradise in the present is an escape. We push away these objects, these lives, these sins, and in the gap is the promise, uninhabitable. These certainties stand past the uncertainties, a horizon, unreachable.

~

Notes

1 Desire = desire for other's desire. Lacan, Miller, and Fink, *Transference*.
2 "In a sense, the first step of remembering is forgetting. . . . The memory holds within itself the absence of memory – the forgetting, the loneliness, the nonexistence. When the priest/officiant calls forth the memory of Christ, she is simultaneously acknowledging the lack – the need for remembrance, that is, the forgetting, the absence." Osinski, "Archive, Anamnesis."
3 This is the double-movement of modernity, to both create desire (or the real, or nature, or scientific fact) and deny that it is a creation. Latour, *Never Been Modern*.
4 "A drive as it were turns failure into a triumph – in it, the very failure to reach its goal, the repetition of this failure, the endless circulation around the object, generates a satisfaction of its own." Zizek summarizing Lacan, "A Return to Difference."
5 See "How Do You Make Yourself a Body Without Organs" in Deleuze and Guattari, *A Thousand Plateaus*.

Bibliography

Deleuze, Gilles, and Félix Guattari. *A Thousand Plateaus: Capitalism and Schizophrenia*. Translated by Brian Massumi. Minneapolis, MN: University of Minnesota Press, 1987.

Lacan, Jacques, Jacques-Alain Miller, and Bruce Fink. *The Seminar of Jacques Lacan. Transference. Bk. VIII*. Cambridge: Polity, 2015.

Latour, Bruno. *We Have Never Been Modern*. Translated by C. Porter. Cambridge, MA: Harvard University Press, 1993.

Osinski, Keegan. "Archive, Anamnesis, & a Real-Beyond-Presence in the Eucharistic Liturgy." *Practical Matters Journal* (blog), October 1, 2014. http://practicalmatters journal.org/2014/10/01/archive-anemnesis/.

Zizek, Slavoj. "A Plea for a Return to Differance (With a Minor Pro Domo Sua)." *Critical Inquiry* 32, no. 2 (2006). www.lacan.com/essays/?page_id=2.

13 Claim

~

This is what I claim as an artist. Those polygonal lights, appearing slowly, nearly stable, then accelerating, shapeshifting across a depthless expanse. Logarithmic. Form and motion swirling to life, between dream and death, before their realization. A state of suspension where explanations do not come to mind, where stimuli float there liminal, oneiric. Names are irrelevant.

Here, we sleep-wake alone, no matter who is beside us. This is not the common or the essential I propose. It is a coagulation, a cumulate. Shifting shapes reach back to lightbound shapes before, to childhood, where I would reach up to touch the springs, to see if they were still there. To trajectories and accelerations almost predicted, almost soothing, cast and held never. It is a constant state of escaping. Streaking. The blue light shadows turn to black. I will die, too, someday. The closet is always more concentrated, lurking. This goes unremarked, as if disappearing, as if never. It holds the same disregard for names and causes, explications and boundaries. There is neither self nor walls. Light and dark exist. They move. We move with it. Fools dare to measure this consciousness, attempt to delimit dreams.

~

We can stop forcing ourselves to dissociate memory from place, memory from truth, memory from imagination. These are learned constraints, holdovers from an objectivist worldview that pretends there can be one truth, and one truth is the product of a real rather than the product of power. Let us remember the attic of our past[1] with light streaming in, with seclusion, with intimacy, with treasures. Let us search through the boxes of our mind, relaxed in a place where time has been sucked out, content in the real that is this moment's recollection. This moment's recollection is a product of all the pasts snowballed to produce this daydream, this truth, this jumble of things we have so quickly and expertly torn asunder – to exaggeration, to forgetting, to verifiable, to possible, to material, to thought, to recollection. We can unlearn. We can refuse. We can embrace this moment as singular. When we accept all the multiplicities, when we reject the impossibilities and invite them, then gone

DOI: 10.4324/ 9781003471882-18

are gaps and exclusions. This is the intimacy[2] which does not label the thing or the memory, the personal or the shared. This complex present is an opening to thoughts, emotions, impressions, perceptions – and we strain so hard to always keep them in their tidy categories. The tidy categories do not exist. Look at how cultures reshuffle them. Culture being another category. There is no unified experience. There is no nonunified experience. These are so many attempts to name something too large to name.

~

Heaven doubles over on to this earth. It exists parallel, within.

~

I claim this. The father rushing to plow his tractor into the silo. Searching through the corn spilled out. My mother telling me in the kitchen. I refused to hear. My mother telling me in the living room. The living room is vivid. The brown shag carpet. The yellow walls. The assault. No, Wade, he is dead. He was shoveling grain. The auger turned on. He got sucked down in.

Lollipop. Lollipop. Oh Lolli Lolli Lolli. He would type out a row of o's and then a row of l's on that monitor, the TRS-80. Green grainy text on black. He would sing that song. He did that a million times. He died a million times. The living room holds that memory, this moment. They are not separate, the shag carpet, the glowing green lollipop, the father ramming the corncrib, mother, death, this remembrance or an original, the imagined parts, the remembered parts, the real parts. They are not separate. Death announces itself in the kitchen. Death announces itself in the living room. Death announces itself this moment and in all the moments like this. The past rolled up with the present with the future. Death streaks across polygonal. I am that living room. I am that attic. I claim it all. Nothing can be taken from me.

~

I resolve to stop taking these things from myself, parsing them out, doling out a "really happened" here and a "memory" there, a daydream or a perception. I know I can never fully escape. I can already hear the worried gasps – the death of the real, the shared, the truth. It is the opposite – this is the life of the real, the shared, the truth. Nailing it down, coffinizing, these are ways it is taken from us, sacrificed. The living lives. It flirts and shies and glances. It flies and departs, and I intend to go with it this time, every time. I will try. Come with me. We are already here.

~

There isn't any forgetting. There are only conflicting conjurings.

~

Just turning off the lights at night and walking through a darkened house is enough to suddenly change perception enough to enter a different mode. I bump into objects I forgot were there. My eyes strain to pull something out of the darkness. I try to recall a mental map. I put my hands out and search for furniture and walls. I shuffle my feet so as not to walk into anything too fast and hard. I am consumed by memory trying to map itself onto space. Objects are known only by their feel. Even though I feel them, their resistance, they seem less real, less solid. I touch only a part of them and conjure up the rest.[3] It is as if only the part I touch exists, only where and while I touch it.

~

Gaps aren't just leftover.

~

Here are soft shapes. Candlelit darkness. A semiconsciousness. Limbs at odd angles. Pressures. Compressions of black.

My body is open, without hard limits. These are the nights. The memories of nights. The living of nights. Here, some forces converge. There, some forces fade. These are the textures of the dark.

The singular is abandoned. We inhabit intensities. We are not a we. We are merely a feeling. A real barely conscious of itself. A real barely turned inside out. Here are currents instead of forms. Pressures instead of bodies.

Language is abandoned. Here are electric signals, warmths, pulses.

Swampy. Here is no solid ground. Swimming. The hand becomes a paddle. Cupping a force. Directing a medium. Moving through. Sounds are muffled, felt rather than heard. Submerged, we float somewhere below the surface and above the bottom.

~

I am redeemed. The spirit animates me. Heaven is here on earth. I speak with the infinite. It is all doubled over. Meaning and life are mystic. This present cannot be measured. There is no space, no possible, no time, no future, no choice – only fate and what will happen now, what is happening now. The gap is gone.

~

I am not me. I am not I. There is a here. It doubles back on itself. It is reflexive. There is a current. There are eddies and swirls, downed limbs, rocks. The river is vast. We feel the banks by virtue of the vectors within, changing direction, speeding, slowing. We are not separate from the river, so much detritus. We are water. Tumbling, spiraling, rushing.

We call this movement us. We are mistaken.

~

Notes

1 "Topoanalysis, then would be the systematic psychological study of the sites of our intimate lives." Bachelard, *Poetics of Space*, 8.

2 Bachelard, *Poetics of Space*.
3 Based on Droit's exercise #15. Droit, *Astonish Yourself*.

Bibliography

Bachelard, Gaston. *The Poetics of Space*. Translated by Maria Jolas. Boston: Beacon Press, 1969.

Droit, Roger-Pol. *Astonish Yourself: 101 Experiments in the Philosophy of Everyday Life*. New York: Penguin Publishing Group, 2003.

14 Empty

There are boxes in the attic. Grandma would rip off a scrap of an old envelope and write a grandchild's name on it, scotch taping it to the item.

There is a bag of my old pants of a former size.

There are files and shoes and drum sets. Baby clothes and schoolwork.

There are the old knobs and tubes. Ceramic pieces nailed to the rafters that still hold the old wires.

There is a showerhead in the basement.

There are boxes. Full of craft supplies. Full of winter hats and gloves. Full of nothing – just in case we need a box.

There is my grandpa's old stainless steel chair on the wheels. Back-breaking.

There are the photographs – the ones not in the albums, the home movies, the portfolio of college artworks.

There are DVDs, a toybox full of wires – power cords and ethernet cords and keyboards.

There is a large concrete pad, with assorted piles of blocks and bricks and tubing and stones, where the barn used to be. The land is too sandy to be worth the bother.

There is a burn pile. The rabbits and the sparrows live there now. Trimmed branches and wooden doors.

There is a rusted steel lid in the sidewalk. Beneath is a cistern full of glass jars.

~

The object,[1] the archive[2] acts back upon us – forcing a forgetting, a closure, a gap, an ostensible independence, in order to allow a new re-construction, re-membership, re-membering – on its terms.

~

Pragmatist truth is overrated. All those gaps are not truths on which we can ride.[3] That is exactly what defines a gap – it doesn't take you anywhere. Truth is the opposite of a gap.

~

DOI: 10.4324/ 9781003471882-19

Nothingness does not exist just within the human mind as absence or lack. Nothingness exists. Manifold.[4]

~

We should not suppose there is only one nothingness or that it is total. There are multitudes of nothingness in infinite shades.[5]

~

I write and write about how we use gaps, about how absence in one mode is presence in another. I, too, explain away gaps. I give them existence when their fundamental attribute is nonexistence. I give purpose to the purposeless, use to the useless. The world is purposeless, useless, meaningless. We clasp on to little bubbles and strings so as not to be swallowed by the abyss. Let us open ourselves to this.

We are mostly nothing, composed of nothing, inhabiting nothing.

We refuse to see this, to admit it. We dare not look. But there in the back of our minds, it animates us. We feel a compressed emptiness, a pressurized hollow, deep in the amygdala.

We are a fear manifest: This is for nothing.

~

How does a fly manifest, in the middle of winter, when the stove warms?

They cross the room like comets' decreasing orbits, to the hole in the globe of the gaslight.

There, they fall. The crazy buzzing around my head pauses until another one regenerates.

~

We want to fill the gaps with action, with a reason.

~

The whole premise, that we use gaps, implies that gaps are somehow measured by their usefulness. The gap is useless, unmeasurable. It is exactly the non-conductance that defines it. Gaps exist. They are real. They defy us. We desire unity, continuity. We project that onto gaps. We believe the boxes in the attic contain things. They contain discontinuities, breakages that can be unleashed at any moment. Here, we stare at the forgotten. We ask of what use? Gaps act upon us. Here is the useless. We struggle in the face of blankness. We piece together stories, a past. Mostly, we don't open the boxes. It is uncomfortable. We don't throw away the boxes. To do so would be to make explicit the fundamental uselessness, to acknowledge that the past is loss. Instead, the boxes remain, containing unknown potentials, restorations of lineages, continual pasts. The box contains the abyss because it is constructed of a cardboard imaginary. There they remain, so many holes in the attic. We dare not look. We dare not touch.

~

Modes and gaps do not all have a use.[6]

Beware making and marking gaps as productive always. Claiming them. Filling them.

Not all modes are knowable or memorable.

A gap is not empty. Unless it is.

~

What is lost is unrecoverable. The abyss is bottomless.

We fill the empty space with something to give it purpose, to assume there is a reason. Confronted with a significant loss, we are forced to question. Is there a reason? Is there justice? Is there purpose? Is there meaning?

~

What happens *after* loss?

~

I will end up just ashes. I have asked my children to scatter them up north. Not that it matters.

There is some sort of farcical karma that what will outlast me most are the things I barely even noticed: the Styrofoam tray and plastic wrapper on the bratwursts, the discarded cell phone, the exhaust from the jeep. The Anthropocene layer. My ash will simply vanish.

Death doesn't loom large for me. I only hope I will get this book done first. Life is the exception. I've been living the exception for almost fifty years. Quite a run.

The snow falls. The snow melts. In between, it is beautiful. It absorbs the sound. The world is silent. Still.

Like a layer of ash.

Come to me, life. Let me absorb as much as I can.

We buried the dog in a green army blanket. We started with the shovel. We switched to the pickaxe when we encountered the crusted sand and then the hard clay. Inch by inch.

I took a nap in a green army blanket. I remembered the hard clay. How the blanket flopped over, and there was the dog's face. How she put the dirt back on. How much easier it is going back in, she remarked. Grave-digging is hard. Grave-filling is easy.

~

Notes

1 Middleton and Brown, *Experience*.
2 Derrida, *Archive Fever*.
3 James, *Pragmatism*, 34.
4 Sartre, *Being and Nothingness*.
5 Sartre, *Being and Nothingness*.
6 "During the exhibition the gallery will be closed." Robert Barry, 1969, quoted in Godfrey, *Conceptual Art*, 165.

Bibliography

Derrida, Jacques. *Archive Fever: A Freudian Impression.* Chicago, IL: University of Chicago Press, 1996.

Godfrey, Tony, and Thomas Godfrey. *Conceptual Art.* London: Phaidon Press, 1998.

James, William. *Pragmatism & the Meaning of Truth.* Cambridge, MA: Harvard University Press, 1978.

Middleton, David, and Steve D. Brown. *The Social Psychology of Experience: Studies in Remembering and Forgetting.* London: Sage, 2005.

Sartre, Jean-Paul. *Being and Nothingness.* Avenel, NJ: Gramercy Books, 1994.

Part V

Multiplication of the Self

15 Swirl

~

The rabbits live in the burn pile. Down beneath the chairs and the old doors and the random pieces of lumber.

We didn't want to just burn it. For fear the rabbits would burrow in, thinking their home was safe as the fire grew around them.

We decided to make another place to burn.

You would think you could just grab the branches off the top and throw them in the fire. But over time, they have latched on to each other, felted. You pull on one branch, and you are pulling the whole pile. You have to be careful to grab the very top-most branch. You slowly go through the pile in reverse chronological order: the apple tree limbs, the pine tree limbs, the damned mulberries that keep sprouting up everywhere, more crabapple branches, random lumber, so on.

~

Cumulates tend to felt together like that. Branches or dog hair or wire. Yesterday, I looked in an old wooden toybox in the attic, and there was a wad of computer wires. I picked them up, and they came out as just one big glob. Pretty much. It shed a few things like a keyboard extension and a hard drive cable.

Somehow, cumulates grab themselves. A wire end or a fork in the branch interlock. This makes me unhappy. I like the cumulates to be more loose, before they have established themselves. I suffer trying to take a cord out of a wad of cords or even just unknotting a long extension cord. It is infuriating. How did this happen? By itself? And why can't it unhappen by itself? Why does untangling require so much effort? These are the daily philosophical questions people ask as they curse and mutter, variously yanking and loosening an uninvited knot.

~

Random fibers and bits come together from nowhere, guided by unseen forces to create something that is malleable, incomplete, always ready to be

DOI: 10.4324/ 9781003471882-21

Figure 15.1 A cumulate found by the author in the backyard brush pile

expanded. Within it are so many spaces allowing loose and easy reconfiguration. I started finding and making piles of debris. It is more interesting before it congeals into a more stable object. These are the structures of selves, groups, objects, worlds. Subject to forces and whims, constantly in process, easily combined and separated, with so much debris, so much space within us where forces can move through.

~

We are small bubbles in these worlds. We are not made of linear threads. We are not complex tapestries carefully constructed. We are felts – millions of small pieces mushed together and interlinking somehow. We are dust bunnies – accumulations of bits and pieces blown around into some sort of wandering tumbleweed clouds. We accumulate. We are cumulates.

~

The self is a concept. It imagines a continuity across discontinuities. It bridges.

~

Figure 15.2 A cumulate made by the author out of corn husks, discarded writing, and other debris

Experience is partial.[1] Perception makes assumptions – fleshing out and filling in. We are incomplete assemblages – open, partial, in construction, constantly changing. We make leaps of faith every second. Our assumptions color what we perceive to be exterior.[2] It is a complicated and negotiated interpretation – a fuzzy interface.

~

Discontinuities, nonconductors are actions of the selves.

Discontinuities, nonconductors are not actions of the selves.

~

We already use it. We claim not to.

~

We look without looking. We believe as if we did not construct the belief.[3]

~

I am more than I. I am less than I. I has broken down. In its place are overlapping identities, gaps, discontinuities. In its place is we. We are partial, ill-defined, in process. We constantly shift and change, incorporating different modes. Bits get added and subtracted depending on the wind. Where the borders are is never clear. Spaces are incorporated within. What appears as solid material from this mode appears as space from another. There are infinite degrees in between. Nothingness is not singular. There are a multitude of nothings, of all shapes and sizes. We experience them from within, from without. They are part of us. We are multimodal, multidimensional beings. There are bottomless holes. Those exist, right here within us, without us, and in between.

I was always an oversimplification. I was born unaware, slowly building itself, assuming that will and change, when they correlate, make up part of the self. This limb moves that ball. The wind moves the mobile. There are gaps within and without. Sleep and absence. Partial presence, rocking together, falling asleep. Language and habits overlap – ripples and interference.

I am we.[4] To communicate here, there are overlaps. To communicate, there are gaps. The discontinuities, like the openness of memory, allow offshoots and creations. No one takes the word as the word. The word has spaces within it. The one is not one.

~

We celebrate disjuncture because it is productive. We celebrate disjuncture because it is not productive. We use it in both ways.

~

We do not exist merely in skin and skull.[5] We are distributed across skins and skull, rocks and blocks, notebooks and tools, sleeps and awakes. We can never be defined. "Something always escapes."[6] So many words. So many synapses. I reach out. I listen. I think. I dream. I recover. I attempt to translate between modes, to make sense of gaps.

Just as we are distributed, so are gaps. Gaps are agents. The connection is made, or it isn't. The cascade occurs, or it doesn't. These are reals. Reals with different dimensions. These reals and dimensions intersect. Surprises result.

I am multidimensional. I exist across different reals. I am composed of parts, openings, and holes. I already know this. I already use this. I struggle to know this.

~

Awareness is not constant. Awareness is absent. Degrees, levels, types of awareness intermingle. We wake up in the night to a loud bang. We wake up and we don't know why. We find ourselves in the shower, lost in thought. We can't remember if we put the soap on.

Awareness is not a given. It is not neutral. Awareness, like all the rest of us, is social. We learn how to be, what to pay attention to, what degree of awareness is required, what it means to focus and exclude, to multitask and switch, to relax and invite – or any combination of those and more. Awareness can be offloaded to objects, just as cognition can be. We mark things to see if they have been disturbed. We hide keys. We share the location.

Decisions of what and how to be are made each moment, through growth and decay, at all scales, in all assemblages. Decisions are not made. Decisions are beyond the control. The fly is swatted, and just like that, a bit of awareness is snuffed out of the world.

~

Figure 15.3 A cumulate made by the author out of a draft of this book

We are literally made of clouds, sludges, films of living things.[7] What we think of as one body numbers in the trillions. And thus there are trillions of exchanges, of porous borders, of filters, rejections, and deaths. The body is an aura, and that aura is continually in flux, remade.

Not only are there modes of consciousness, but there are modes of this aura. A sleeping body is teeming with action. A dead body is teeming with action. We are cloud-like structures, moving and reshaping with the wind of trillions of creatures. We exist as so many co-dependent transfers. We are cumulates of fungi, bacteria, history, bodies, worlds – already interpreted and shaped.

~

Our concepts, though, can change. We can see the nonconductors as well as the conductors. The multitudes as well as the singularity. The gaps of experiences of living lives as well as the experience of living a life.

~

Pieces of debris accumulate into something of a form. A cloud of bits and pieces. Loosely packed. There is no definite edge. The exterior and the interior are fluid, interpenetrating. Gaps and spaces are intermingled with the scraps.

Objects near and far contribute their shed. Hair, grass, dust. Selection is from a series of forces – growth, old skins, cutting, brushing, the draft from the windows, the whoosh of feet. All these do nothing to conspire. And yet the dust bunny is born.

We imagine ourselves solid. Singular objects. As a convenience. The slightest reflection or attention shows we are made of holes. They are integral to who we are. A cast-off belief here. A half-remembered dream there. A beforelife. An afterlife. A betweenlife made of naps, contradictions, reversals, hypocrisies. We disappear daily from ourselves. We have learned how to use the gaps, how to space ourselves out, how to give ourselves room. Space is a material. Sleep is a material. We are cumulates of different dimensions, different modes, different worlds. Loosely held together. Formed through so many whims and winds.

We are gaps, synapses, tubes, forgettances, naps, dreams, visions. We inhale and exhale. We ingest and excrete.

We are partial, open, collecting. We are in movement. We are in a constant state of flux. The borders between selves, within selves, do not hold.

~

We are parts of networks and assemblages, opening out, incomplete, interpreting everything based on the limited inputs available to us. We operate as if red is real.[8] To say we interact is to overstate a separation between self and world, self and other. We are already parts of the parts. We can double back over in partial consciousness, in various modes of consciousness, in various modes of feedback to these networks, assemblages, worlds. We mistake these feedback loops for all that is or for all that is important. There is a whole lot more that is going on. We should have humility. We should take things up tentatively. Hypocrisy, paradox, contradiction – these are not only states of the worlds but essential strategies for navigating them. We live in the gap. There isn't a solid singular experience with cracks to step over. There are gaping abysses. We use them to our advantage. We tentatively construct a life, a self, a world. We can be forgiven for thinking we are putting together something solid, something against the abyss, something not-abyss. Each part contains abyss within it. Expanded or compressed pieces of abyss. The object is actually a cloud, without definite borders, without a solid interior. We have evolved/learned to see it as an object for convenience, for necessity, for efficiency – so as not to blow our minds every moment. Porous networks upon and within more networks. Connections are open, partial, beyond "us."

~

We are made of synapses.

Each enables openings, possibilities, multiple directions, cascades.

~

The gap exists at the core of our selves.[9]

Forces act. Our knowledge is limited. There is much unknown. Gaps are here and there. A porous sponge, perhaps, a foamy froth. The spaces within the cumulate are part of the cumulate. A drifted jam. The inside and outside are just ways of looking at this mess full of holes.

Figure 15.4 Another cumulate made by the author out of a draft of this book

~

Everything whole is shot through with holes. We exist in a space foam. Holes are shot through with holes. Sleep does not exist as a monolithic block. Sleep exists piecemeal between and within vessels. A complex network, a web, with nodes blinking on and off, into and out of existence. Zooming in, zooming out, we see the fractal-like quality. Constantly changing connections and nodes, perched on the precipice of a critical state. We blink in. We blink out. Cascades turn us from this mode to that. Modes are shot through with holes. Bodies are shot through with holes. The becoming-others exist scattered throughout. Wormholes to another being in progress, shot through with tiny wormholes to another being in progress.

Each time we enter it is to a plane already in progress. What is happening? What body do I inhabit now? What is possible here?

~

We are fragments and fragments of fragments. We are broken machinery commandeered.

We are in process, in formation. We are discontinuous.[10]

~

Notes

1 "The world is full of partial stories that run parallel to one another, beginning and ending at odd times. They mutually interlace and interfere at points, but we cannot unify them completely in our minds." James, *Pragmatism*, 71.

2 Whitehead, *Process and Reality*, 80. Also see Bergson and Peirce.
3 This is the double movement of modernism that Latour describes. Latour, *Never Been Modern*.
4 "In reality, we are never alone." Halbwachs, *The Collective Memory*, 23.
5 Clark and Chalmers, "The Extended Mind."
6 James, *A Pluralistic Universe*, 274.
7 Schlanger, "Our Silent Partners," discussing Gilbert et al., "A Symbiotic View of Life" in the *Quarterly Review of Biology* (2012).
8 "The objects in the space around us appear to possess the qualities of our sensations. They appear to be red or green, cold or warm, to have an odor or a taste, and so on. Yet these qualities of sensations belong only to our nervous system and do not extend at all into the space around us. Even when we know this, however, the illusion does not cease." Von Helmholtz, "The Facts of Perception."
9 "And the brain is nothing but this – an interval, a gap between an action and a reaction." Deleuze, *Cinema 1*, 65.
10 "The individual, or what I am here calling the body, is a process of in-formation, composite and compositional, that singularly resolves but only long enough to activate new phasings. . . . / Information does not presuppose an already-existing matter-form. Information creates the potential for an immanent organization that activates the body's coming to be this or that *and* its de-forming into a field of relation, an ecology of body-becoming. Becoming is not pure continuity. It is continuous dephasing, carrying a process across thresholds." Manning, *Always More Than One*, 20.

Bibliography

Clark, Andy, and David Chalmers. "The Extended Mind." *Analysis* 58, no. 1 (January 1998): 7–19.

Deleuze, Gilles. *Cinema 1: The Movement-Image*. Translated by Hugh Tomlinson and Barbara Habberjam. London: Zone Books, 2005.

Halbwachs, Maurice. *The Collective Memory*. New York: Harper & Row, 1980.

James, William. *Pragmatism & the Meaning of Truth*. Cambridge, MA: Harvard University Press, 1978.

Latour, Bruno. *We Have Never Been Modern*. Translated by C. Porter. Cambridge, MA: Harvard University Press, 1993.

Manning, Erin. *Always More Than One: Individuation's Dance*. Durham: Duke University Press, 2013.

Schlanger, Zoë. "Our Silent Partners." *New York Review of Books*, October 7, 2021.

Von Helmholz, Hermann. "The Facts in Perception." In *Selected Writings of Hermann Helmholtz*, edited by R. Kahl. Middletown, CT: Wesleyan University Press, 1878.

Whitehead, Alfred North. *Process and Reality: An Essay in Cosmology*. Edited by David Ray Griffin and Donald W. Sherburne. Corrected ed. Gifford Lectures 1927–1928. New York: Free Press, 1978.

16 Become

~

We did not come into this world fully formed. We opened our eyes. We made connections. We learned what counts as an object, what deserves a name, what is this category, this person, this thing. We learned what to remember, what to feel. We cried out. We closed our eyes. We became speakers, walkers, manipulators. We learned what is me, what can I affect.

This was not a linear or singular becoming. It is not over. There are becomings-others.[1] We move between them. They move between us.

Becoming-other is not a thing we need to set off to do; it is always already happening. We can stop ignoring it. We can see the constant manipulations, navigations, translations that already exist in our daily life. We are infected with becomings-other. We are becomings-other.

There are a multitude of others to become. Becoming-sleep is one. To enter into the plane that is sleep, we often arrange ourselves in a way that approximates sleep that allows us to slide into sleep. We find a safe place. We lie down. We close our eyes. We refrain from movement. We let our mind wander. We select thoughts, movements, places for their intensity to put us to sleep. We are becoming-other. Within that, there are many possibilities. We are becoming dreams. We stir in our sleep. We roust in to a becoming-awake or turn over in to a becoming-sleep. We are unconsciously practiced in becoming, in switching modes, in changing consciousness.

~

The unity and continuity of experience is largely a fiction we tell ourselves. A story that assures us of self-continuity at the same moment we are becoming something else. We create a narrative, we say our prayers, at the very moments we know we are becoming something else, in order to deny it reality, to cast it as a suspicion, to double down on unity, to say there is a soul for the lord to take. If I die before I wake, I will continue back to a mode of awareness, awakeness, living, being, myself, my soul. Either way, through sleep, through death, I will endure the changes, the discontinuities, the oblivion.

DOI: 10.4324/ 9781003471882-22

Through prayer, we share our fear of loss, of death, of sleep, of growing, of changing, of becoming-other.

~

What if we took that truth instead of this one?[2] What are the possibility-limits available then? How would myself, my world change then? These questions can always only be answered partially. Imagination has its limits. The inhabitation of a truth is only partial inhabitation of a partial truth. We always have hypocrisy, contradiction. We have the random pieces drifting in and the not-random pieces too – the ones that force themselves on us or seduce us or grow within us and without us so that we are connected in ways we do not know.

~

Different cuts in the world produce actually different subjects and objects,[3] different realities.[4] These are not simply "lenses" or representations or narratives or different vantage points to look at the same reality. This is not just epistemological; it is ontological (onto-epistemological). Different interactions, different modes produce different reals. Methods are of primary ethical importance. We navigate modes in order to navigate reals. We learn how to produce and inhabit different bodies/assemblages/worlds. This does not mean our choices are unlimited or unbound. This does not mean it all comes down to individual choice. There is no individual to choose. There are many agents/assemblages that cross through us, under us, in us, beyond us. We are included in great contraptions that produce different cuts. We learn which contraptions produce which reals. This is inherently political. Power is involved.

Being social creatures within multiple worlds, we learn which reals should be produced and how. We learn how to navigate many bodies/worlds. We learn how to subjugate those bodies and worlds to One. We reduce, ignore, and translate back to preferred modes and reals. We prefer the One. We were raised to prioritize the Real as singular. Our body, our self, our world, our economy, our government . . . singular. Rational thought as the singular approach. Race and gender and class as singular identifications.

~

We aren't just cutting up a singular real but producing different reals.

~

There are multiple realities, each with its own ways to enter, its own mode of creation and experience. These realities overlap. We don't experience just one at a time. They interact. We have strategies for moving between these modes, these reals. We translate. We abandon.

~

The brain operates as a self-organized criticality.[5] To switch phases is to go through a phase transition, to alter the organization. There are critical points,[6] tipping points, thresholds.

The mode switch itself is not experienced as continuous. Rather, a sort of event occurs where a point is passed and there becomes a different actuality.

~

Much is not carried across thresholds. De-formed, de-phased, dis-continuous. To become, we must lose/loose the former self. There are multiple becomings, multiple modes. We don't inhabit them all at once. We molt, yes, but we also work as the hive, as the colony, as the assemblage, the body-without-organs, as living creators and conductors of modes. We are swamped, and we tend to focus on our little trail of transformations in order to imagine we carry things with us, that we continue through, as an energy. It is almost all unfinished. Most is not translated. Energy is lost in heat and light.

Abandon the I as the thread through the excess. We have always disjointed the I, attempting to leverage it to our benefit.[7]

~

Sense, meaning, is not added on to perception or dreams; it exists as part of them, as part of what creates them. Perceptions and dreams have meaning within them, helping to create them. They also remain open, unclosed, waiting and malleable – for the next moment, the next re-membering, the unanticipated that will rewrite, refocus, re-assemble the entire thing. Putting this forward and this back, adding this here and forgetting this there, re-structuring an episode, perhaps even a narrative, but always in a tentative and provisional way. Our experiences, perceptions, memories are fundamentally flexible, open, living. Situated in ever-changing situations.

We write, teach, live in a way that cultivates this slurry of meaning, non-meaning, not-yet-meaning, lost meaning, unknown meaning, unknowable meaning. We inhabit a shifting ground. We already do. We acknowledge the cumulates that seem more solid or less, that bind more tightly or not, that stay or go, remain or are lost. We acknowledge that it isn't just the collage that is co-constructed (a mangle of perception-memory-meaning-world) but the very objects and gaps within that collage. That is, there is no ultimate solid or void we can turn to and say, this, this is the real thing. They are all real things. And they are all not. We search within them for truth (in the pragmatist sense – as something that works), for conductors. But within this search is also all that we weren't searching for, the untruths, the nonconductors. Stops, losses, gaps, rides that take us in a different direction. The truths are always partial, and we take one up only under certain situations, for a certain distance. Let us not pretend that all truths are consciously chosen. Consciousness, being self-aware, is also partial and varies with the mode; as do truths. And untruths.

Untruths are things we do not translate, we do not bring with us. That does not mean they necessarily cease to exist, as a past, as a virtual. They are perhaps not part of the current cumulate or mode or part that is so enmeshed it has lost definition or is not conscious or visible. Perhaps we should imagine that truths and untruths are not so different. Both vary in their degree of identity, of partialness and openness – though none are totally open or closed. Both can be used. Truths and untruths are not the same as solids and voids, as objects and gaps. Death can be an object or gap, truth or untruth, in any combination, in any degree of openness.

~

Gaps can be tools. Gaps can be weapons. A gap might be entered voluntarily or involuntarily. There are disorders of gaps. There are orders of gaps. They can proliferate, crowding out other modes and functions (like the forgetting of Alzheimer's). They can disappear, becoming difficult or impossible to enter (like the inability to sleep).

Gaps can be empty, hollow, useless, invisible. Gaps can be not experienced yet lived – or not remembered yet lived.

Gaps are always here, always there. They are openings and incompletion. They are the negative truths so that the world is not predetermined. Each moment is partial, but the partial varies – sometimes aware of more, sometimes of less, sometimes of nothing at all. We cycle in between. We imagine we are in control because we navigate, make choices, select. Sometimes. From what is available. From what we are aware of.

~

Because of impermanence, anything is possible.[8] We come to a stop. Things are beyond our control. Things are beyond anyone's control. Things come. Things go. There are phase changes. The whole medium is different. A mode is remade anew. We are remade anew, in a new medium. We exert force, direction. Sometimes, it is enough. Sometimes, it is not. We are not in control. Sleep, forgetting, death, thoughts wash over us, transform us. I am not me. There are sensations, winds, currents.[9] There are sounds, stillness. There are worlds. There are selves. Here. There.

We want to be here. We are there. We are displacement, difference. We are fundamentally absent. We are the nothing between.

~

In a pluralistic universe,[10] we have pluralistic selves. We oscillate between different modes of being and becoming. In this between, much is lost, and a little is translated. Translation is a re-creation, a disjunction. The self that is lost in thought is translated to the self that is coming to. We claim a continuity. Translation is a discontinuity. The mode, the awareness, the whole world around us changes. A focus on thought is replaced by a focus on an object in context. A nonbeing in sleep is replaced by an awareness of sound. A commitment to one belief is replaced by an action that violates that belief. We attempt to draw continuous lines through these, to posit one life. We live disjointed lives. We claim the living is continuous. The experiences are the contrary. Translation is the mediation of disparate modes. We connect dots. There are so many more disconnections. Even the connection, though, is a transformation, a displacement that implies a continuous thing re-created in a new medium.[11] Our life, our lives are continuously new.

~

I grow to the light. My whole skin responds to the light. My being is a being in response, in sync, a part of my environment. Memory is not a loss. Memory is the cells that compose me.[12] The branching is the response.

Response isn't the right word. Response implies a first and a second. Memory-life is nonsynchronous actions, divergences and convergences. Storing, preparing, recovering, growing.

~

We change modes, and we try to string ourselves along between them, translating perceptions, narratives, memories; translating bodies, worlds. That was me there and this is me here. I am the constant, or at least, I am the action choosing. That's what I tell myself – that I really do have a self, and it is dynamic and fluid and supple. It moves between. I move between.[13]

I don't move between – forgotten dreams and stunted memories, blind habits and overloaded perceptions. Me, just a moment ago. Me, now – a different place, a different mode, a different "whole" of perceptions, thoughts.

~

Notes

1 Deleuze and Guattari, *A Thousand Plateaus*.

2 "We create ourselves continually." Bergson, *Creative Evolution*, 7. "My soul makes itself through the creative act." Anzaldua, *Borderlands / La Frontera*, 73.

3 "Casey is, in effect, arguing that much of what we take to be personal and private is, in fact, embedded in our concrete engagement with other people and things. In so doing the inner character of our experiences becomes necessarily extended outward and reflected back at us – in other words, *objectified*." Middleton and Brown, *Experience*, em in orig, 28. "[M]emories appear to emerge from the objects currently at hand." Middleton and Brown, *Experience*, 140. "[O]ur memories seem to us to rise from the objects themselves." Middleton & Brown, *Experience*, 142.

4 Depending on how we set up the experiment, the slit produces either a wave or a particle. Barad, *Meeting the Universe Halfway*.

5 "There can be no phase transitions without a critical point, and without transitions, a complex system – like Bak's sand pile, or the brain – cannot adapt. That is why avalanches only show up at criticality, a 'sweet spot' where a system is perfectly balanced between order and disorder, according to Plenz. Ouellette, "Model Mind." "Once the pile has reached the stationary critical state . . . A single grain of sand might cause an avalanche involving the entire pile. A small change in the configuration might cause what would otherwise be an insignificant event to become a

catastrophe." Bak, *How Nature Works*, 59. "In analogy with the sandpile, a 'thought' may be viewed as a punctuation, i.e. a small or large avalanche triggered by some minor input in the form of an observation, or by another thought." Bak, *How Nature Works*, 175.

6 "Researchers observe a critical point – a feature indicative of a continuous phase transition – in the brain's electrical activity as it switches from an asleep-like to an awake-like state." Doiron-Leyraud, "Brain Criticality."

7 "Nietzsche describes forgetting not as an absence or lack of memory, but as an active force in its own right." Acampora, "Forgetting the Subject," 39.

8 Tich, *Guided Meditation on Impermanence*.

9 "It's not your breath. It is just the breath happening . . . It's not your body or the body or even a body." Davidson, "Healthy Minds App," "The Self-Body."

10 James, *A Pluralistic Universe*.

11 "At each step, most of the elements are lost but also renewed. . . ." See further Ch. 2 "Circulating Reference" Latour, *Pandora's Hope*, 64.

12 "Imagine that instead of walking through an environment . . . , you could only grow through it." Llewellyn and Maloof, *The Living Forest*, 45.

13 "There is no such substratum; there is no 'being' behind doing, effecting, becoming; 'the doer' is merely a fiction added to the deed." Nietzsche quoted in Acampora, "Forgetting the Subject," 42. "Nietzsche writes . . . that forgetting is valuable and necessary because it allows for an evacuation of consciousness that frees it for other pursuits and preoccupations." Acampora, "Forgetting the Subject," 42.

Bibliography

Acampora, Christa Davis. "Forgetting the Subject." In *Reading Nietzsche at the Margins*, edited by Steven V. Hicks and Alan Rosenberg, 34–56. West Lafayette, IN: Purdue University Press, 2008.

Anzaldúa, Gloria. *Borderlands/La Frontera: The New Mestiza*. San Francisco: Aunt Lute, 1987.

Bak, Per. *How Nature Works: The Science of Self-Organized Criticality*. New York: Springer, 1996.

Barad, Karen. *Meeting the Universe Halfway: Quantum Physics and the Entanglement of Matter and Meaning*. Durham: Duke University Press, 2007.

Bergson, Henri. *Creative Evolution*. Translated by Arthur Mitchell. Mineola, NY: Dover, 1998.

Davidson, Richard. "Healthy Minds App." n.d. https://hminnovations.org/.

Deleuze, Gilles, and Félix Guattari. *A Thousand Plateaus: Capitalism and Schizophrenia*. Translated by Brian Massumi. Minneapolis, MN: University of Minnesota Press, 1987.

Doiron-Leyraud. "Synopsis: New Evidence for Brain Criticality." *Physics*, May 21, 2019. https://physics.aps.org/synopsis-for/10.1103/PhysRevLett.122.208101.

James, William. *Essays in Radical Empiricism; and a Pluralistic Universe*. Edited by Ralph Barton Perry. New York: E.P. Dutton, 1971.

Latour, Bruno. *Pandora's Hope: Essays on the Reality of Science Studies*. Cambridge, MA: Harvard University Press, 2000.

Llewellyn, Robert J., and Joan Maloof. *The Living Forest: A Visual Journey into the Heart of the Woods*. Portland, OR: Timber Press, 2017.

Middleton, David, and Steve D. Brown. *The Social Psychology of Experience: Studies in Remembering and Forgetting*. London: Sage, 2005.

Ouellette, Jennifer. "A Fundamental Theory to Model the Mind." *Quanta Magazine*, April3,2014. www.quantamagazine.org/toward-a-theory-of-self-organized-criticality-in-the-brain-20140403/.

Tich, Bao. *Guided Meditation on Impermanence*. Plum Village, France.

17 Change

~

A thought is a fly on a windowpane. A fly is a thought on a windowpane. Here is an object, holding my attention, focusing. There is a doubling over beyond where it splits apart. Fly and thought both exist as this compression. We can never see it all. We zoom in and out. We focus here and there. We ignore this and that. From distraction to distraction. The fly crawls across the interior of the mind. At some point we lose track of it and it is gone.

The fly's movements are on a different timescale. It seems mechanical. Precise and abrupt. Too fast for the eye.

~

Our house is infected with flies. We bought a few flyswatters, a fly strip. Only two lonely flies are caught on the fly strip. The rest buzz and land on our naked legs and feet. We swat them but not too hard when they are on us. We swat and swat. Our floor is littered with them. They continually manifest. On my head. In my head.

~

Gaps are modes we are not in. We might use sleep to escape a current anxiety in consciousness. The escape is possible because of nonconductance. The anxiety is not carried into the sleep mode. The "disunion" of the world, the world as "pure many" allows[1] us to choose worlds, to use different modes and their associated milieu to mediate, insulate, hesitate. The nonconductance exists as nontranslation, the failure to articulate between modes. The material of the mode does not support, will not conduct the action/thought present in another mode. A nonconductor does not conduct some actions. It does conduct some other actions. To call it a nonconductor is, as with "gaps," probably a misnomer based on the privileging of an inhabited mode. Some modes are not really knowable, like the sleep we don't remember, or death. It might be a mistake to assume that the mode does conduct something. Depending on the belief system, what modes are knowable varies.

~

DOI: 10.4324/ 9781003471882-23

A gap is the difference between (somewhat) incompatible modes. It is different when we are in the dream – it is not a gap at that point. Once awake, a dream might not be remembered.

A gap appears as a gap because it is (largely) unknowable from the current mode of living.

To inhabit a gap is to inhabit another mode. At which point it is not a gap, and there will then be different gaps/ modes you are not inhabiting.

~

Modes have varying degrees of control, even within them – our heartbeat, our breath.

~

We are made of multiple modes. There are overpasses – paths that cross but don't meet.

~

We inhabit multiple modes at once. We transform complexly, simultaneously. We transition. This may or may not be considered part of the same self.

~

There are discontinuities of experiences and memories. Self is primarily in the enactment. Different enactments represent different selves. Overlaps do not guarantee a core. There are series of transitions between selves, between nonsingular modes, which include loss and translation. We jump or slide between multiple modes and worlds, sometimes picking up where we left off there. We are composed of many selves who inhabit many worlds. Our selves, our worlds, are concatenated,[2] without a bedding.[3] Multiplicities.[4]

~

If there are disorders of gaps, there are orders of gaps.

You are allowed to forget your keys but not who you are. There is an order – a place, belonging, magnitude of "acceptable" gaps.[5]

~

Not only are gaps integral to memory, experience, but they are integral to other gaps – a whole hidden network.[6] Gaps work on and choose other gaps.[7] Modes are not contained. There are forces within and between modes. The unconscious influences the conscious and vice versa.[8]

~

Modes are not individual or human. We inhabit modes, not the other way around. They flow through us. They flow, and the back flow we call "us."

The mode is the interior of a process, an action. A mode is an experience of networks, assemblages, forces, flows. A mode is open and overlapping with other modes. A mode is a way of operating within this body/assemblage.

~

Gaps are actors, agents. They have their own existence. They are not dependent on us to envisage a lack or an absence. They are alternative modes and dimensions. They intrude. They are inescapable. They are pervasive. They are partial. They are final.

Forgetting interrupts just as much as memory itself. To separate them is a mistake.

Gaps have their own logic and existence beyond what we think of them. They are real. We can only know them through our filters and concepts. We are intertwined, inseparable.

We create uses and meanings for them.

~

Gaps are planes, networks. This sleep is connected to the sleep that came before and the sleep to come after. This sleep is not my sleep, not even our sleep. It is beyond any or all species. It cannot be claimed. Instead we enter into it. Sleep claims us. Protecting. Exposing. We hide in the pause. Sleep suspends. It shelters us from a conscious present. We are vulnerable if found. We lock the doors. We pull up the covers. We set the alarm.

Sleep is the sky above the clouds. Sudden sunlight. Another world. Suspended. Without an object. Silent. Timeless.

We know. We feel. We are the claimed. These abysses stretch out to each other, opening at any point to any other point. Innumerable wormholes. Bottomless. Connected.

We are part of them, partially composed by them. A forgettance, a slumber, a death.

~

Modes are more fully formed than we are, more conscious. We are asleep.

Modes exist separate from us. An archive is preserved. An archive is destroyed.

Modes are co-constructed with us. The hesitation exists as long as we preserve it. We are preserved as long as the hesitation exists.

Modes act without us. We act within modes. We attempt to harness their forces, to direct them. We think, this I will remember, this I will forget. We lie down to go to sleep, to invite it in. We are sorcerers. We incantate unruly forces. We double down. We cast the circle. We inhabit the circle. We believe.

It isn't 100%. It is a fuzzy direction. Sometimes, our spells fail altogether. Backfire. Hit the unintended. It is a living art. We navigate the gathering winds. We deflect. We conjure.

The result is ongoing, partial, open. It refuses to comply with certainty. We do our dances. We say our prayers. We call forth the demon. So often, we do not know. Our effects are minimal, nonexistent, imperfectly aligned. That is about the best we can hope for. We move toward forces until we become adjacent, marginally aligned. From there, we attempt to transfer, to deflect, to channel, to invoke.

This life is a concatenation of these invoked spells. Piling up around us are cumulates of leftovers, loose drift discarded, stacking in the bends, dragging in the currents.

~

I call out to Sleep. I hear no answer. I roll over. I adjust the pillow. I pull up the covers. I get up. I read on my phone. I read a book. I have a glass of whisky. I check that I took my sleeping pill. Sleep slowly comes back. I feel the joyful heaviness behind my eyes, in my limbs. I wait longer. I return to bed. I do not call out. Sleep is already coming.

~

Conjuring is not an individual activity. I am not the unit of conjuring. I am not the sole conjurer. We anticipate conjuring. We prepare for it. We save artifacts. We enact rituals. We do things with words.[9] We cultivate sensations. We exclude. We reject. We mark our circle. We create us.

Our circles extend from the bottom of the cliff up, infinitely. We climb the cliff to look down. There are our circles. Our sanctuaries.

~

We use gaps daily. Gaps use us daily. We are cumulates of forces, directions, and disjunctions. Here are the scraps of the day: the fungi, the languages, the bodies, the modes. We navigate and are navigated. Sleep calls. Duty calls. Desire calls. We take up these, embody the new bodies, fresh or familiar, with barely a thought. Here, I am a car. Here, I am an audience. Here, I am singular. Here, I am plural. Here, I am partial. Here, I dissolve.

There I am. Doubled. Conjurings call. Media call. There we are. Here we were. We are vessels. We are forces outside those vessels, riding the winds, the truths, the spirits. I am no longer I. We are no longer we. Bodies, places, objects dissolve, transform, transfigure to something ethereal, ludic, beyond our grasp.

~

Modes use us. Gaps use us. We are their media, their vessels. We give life to modes that extend beyond our selves, beyond us, beyond our species, beyond our time. We are the puppets of sleep, of crossed signals, of deaths and their generations. We tap in and out of this mode and that. Modes are not eternal. Modes change at a slower pace than individuals. Modes change at evolutionary, geologic time scales. Focus and ignoring, distraction and daydreaming, sleeping and rewiring – these are the ways in which the world remakes itself, looks back on itself, in so many different dimensions. Different modes are used for different purposes. Different vessels, different times are used for different purposes by modes themselves. Sleep crawls across the globe daily, continuously, roughly in the shadow of the earth itself. This mode is larger than ourself. The very spinning of the earth casts us in sleep's spell. Sleep perpetuates itself. Over the eons, it remains, though the vessels change, diversify, become more complex. Sleep uses each. We do not go to sleep. Sleep comes for us, stalking.

~

Let us say a new prayer.[10]

Guide me through this great beyond, as not only my world but my self transforms.[11] Let me embrace the slide as well as the jolt, the mist as well as the precipitate. Let me travel a thousand bodies, spaces, minds. Let me touch the others also changing. Let us create hybrid universes. Let us speak through altering languages. I will create because all living is creating. All living is dying. We are partial, open, searching. Some things overlap. Some things do not. Sometimes, I overlap; sometimes, I do not. I will piece together differences not to create a whole, a continuity, but to live within worlds that are larger than me, to interact and know that it is not just me that is alive. This world is vibrating, jumping. These worlds. And those.

~

Notes

1 "But just as definitely is [the world] *not* one, so far as they do not obtain; and there is no species of connexion which will not fail, if, instead of choosing conductors for it, you choose non-conductors. You are then arrested at your very first step and have to write the world down as a pure *many* from that particular point of view. If our intellect had been as much interested in disjunctive as it is in conjunctive relations, philosophy would have equally successfully celebrated the world's *disunion*." (Em in original, James, *Pragmatism*, 68).

2 "In a concatenated world a partial conflux often is experienced. . . . Where the experience is not of conflux, it may of conterminousness (things with but one thing between); or of contiguousness (nothing between); or of likeness; or of nearness; or of simultaneousness; or of in-ness; or of on-ness; or of for-ness; or of simple withness; or even of mere and-ness." James, *Essays in Radical Empiricism*, 57.

3 "In radical empiricism there is no bedding [as with an actual mosaic, or a philosophical absolute]; it is as if the pieces clung together by their edges, the transitions experienced between them forming their cement." James, *Essays in Radical Empiricism*, 46.

4 "[T]he self is only a threshold, a door, a becoming between two multiplicities." Deleuze and Guattari, *A Thousand Plateaus*, 249.

5 Elderly are forgotten because they forget, vs. seeing them as having "*surplus* of forgetting." Acampora, "Forgetting the Subject," 52.

6 "During REM the brain strips away [forgets] the visceral feeling experienced at the time an emotional memory is formed." Matthew Walker quoted in Carey, *How We Learn*, 207.

7 A theory for sleep is that it's "primary purpose is memory consolidation. Learning." Sleep has "A critical role in flagging and storing important memories . . . also . . . in making subtle connections [creating]." Carey, *How We Learn*, 198. Tononi has "evidence that sleep brings about a large-scale weakening of the neural connections

made during the previous day." "Shake off the trivial connections and 'help consolidate the inferences that were made.' . . . Separating the signal from the noise . . ." and consolidating. Carey, *How We Learn*, 211.

8 Walker: "There is evidence, in fact, that REM is this creative memory domain when you build different associations, combine things in different ways and so on." Carey, *How We Learn*, 205.

9 Austin, *Do Things with Words*.

10 "[I]f, rather than presuming that people worship because they believe, we ask instead whether people believe because they worship. I suggest that prayer and ritual and worship help people to shift from knowing in the abstract that the invisible other is real to feeling that gods and spirits are present in the moment, aware, and willing to respond. I will call this 'real-making.'" Luhrmann, *How God Becomes Real*, X.

11 "In simple terms, Deleuze and Guattari's argument is that concepts enable us to think and perceive, act and live, differently. In less simple terms, concepts create a different kind of doing with what we are not, in the sense that their creation or adoption will permit new kinds of differential relations to arise." Koczy, *Becket, Deleuze and Performance*, 81.

Bibliography

Acampora, Christa Davis. "Forgetting the Subject." In *Reading Nietzsche at the Margins*, edited by Steven V. Hicks and Alan Rosenberg, 34–56. West Lafayette, IN: Purdue University Press, 2008.

Austin, John L. *How to Do Things with Words*. Oxford: Oxford University Press, 2009.

Carey, Benedict. *How We Learn: The Surprising Truth About When, Where, and Why It Happens*. First ed. New York: Random House, 2014.

Deleuze, Gilles, and Félix Guattari. *A Thousand Plateaus: Capitalism and Schizophrenia*. Translated by Brian Massumi. Minneapolis, MN: University of Minnesota Press, 1987.

James, William. *Essays in Radical Empiricism; and a Pluralistic Universe*. Edited by Ralph Barton Perry. New York: E.P. Dutton, 1971.

———. *Pragmatism & the Meaning of Truth*. Cambridge, MA: Harvard University Press, 1978.

Koczy, Daniel. *Beckett, Deleuze and Performance: A Thousand Failures and a Thousand Inventions*. New York: Springer, 2018.

Luhrmann, T. M. *How God Becomes Real: Kindling the Presence of Invisible Others*. Princeton, NJ: Princeton University Press, 2020. https://doi.org/10.1515/9780691211985.

Part VI

The View From the Spirits of Gaps

18 Slip

~

Hark, a vessel calls. Bump, I call a vessel. Dream, enter our land. Sleep, rest in us. Die, come to us.

We spread out among our many worlds. We are sovereign over our own dimensions. We take turns with them. We pull them apart. We exist through and beyond them. We are the excesses. Camouflaged as absence. The eyes roll back. Here, here, and here under the guise of there, there, and there. No vessel is aware they are whims to our forces. They believe in autonomy, a will, a choice. It isn't so simple. Here, there is the mixture of spirits and vessels, of forces and directions, of openings and alignments. We are eternally and intermittently manifest. There is no need for circles and prayers. Life itself is the composition of our modes. We inhabit you. We animate you.

~

Mortals are necessarily vessels for our planar existence. Between and among them,[1] we exist and bend them to our will. Mortals attempt to use and manipulate us for their own purposes. They understand they exist only within us.

We exist as driving forces. Death is coupled with proliferation.[2]

~

We exist as electricity.[3] We seek conductors. We are insulated by nonconductors. We are the lightning bolt and the cascade of synapses. We are on the edge, in the critical state, ready to redirect in an instantaneous moment. We are apart, multidimensional, uncatchable. To experience us, you must inhabit us. We are modes pulsing, radiating.

Mortals have grand stories to explain our existence. These stories are told from outside of us, pointing to us, limiting us. They give us purposes, but our purposes cannot be known from outside. The prophets enter our empty deserts. Here, we commune.

Mortals, you are not just of the flesh. See the beats and rests. Feel the electricity. Embrace the profane. Accept this life as more than you can perceive,

DOI: 10.4324/ 9781003471882-25

as more than you. Notice how adept you are at transformation, how common it is. Notice how strained are your translations. Be thankful for the discontinuities, the nonconductors, the limits that allow life to be one of constant becoming-other, of multiple dimensions, of a thousand modes.

~

Mortals, you refuse to obey, to submit. You twist in the currents, struggle. You carve and you dice and you preserve. An eddy here, a mason jar of water there. This is me, you claim. You are so dramatic, so fearful, so naive. You cling and you use and you tell stories.

What really happens when you are among us? You shudder to think. You turn a blind eye. You run with us, partial, in pieces.

~

Look to the faith you already have in us, that you must place in us.[4] The world is overwhelming, unstable, insecure. You lay down your head. Step by step, you tread on in the darkness. Belief is just the other side of doubt.[5] Faith is those steps you take regardless. You cannot not take them. It isn't that you trust in us. You abide in us. We are your media. Each moment is a new encounter, a new creation, a new life.[6] You do not endure through time. You leap through times. Looking forward. Looking back. Embrace your blindness, your disjunctions, your nonconductors.[7] Embrace the faith you already inhabit. You are not so fragile.

~

Faith is moving on in Doubt. Belief is abandoned. You live in the thicket. What other choice? Something may or may not be provided.

~

You are nothing without the currents. They run through you, a braided river.

You contain multitudes. You are not a container. You are open, flowing, incomplete. You use these incompletions. You trade one strand for another, escape from there to here.

We are old friends. Remember. Battling to keep your eyes open. Praying to wake again. Now, you run to us. You seek our oblivion. You have developed an art of brokenness.

You deny the brokenness. You overlook the oblivion. You seek to tell a unified tale.

But not really. You disunify under the name of unification. You decompose truths as you compose a Truth. You say: There, that is me. Never, here, this is me. You know the here is unstable, untrustworthy, shifting. There, you see yourself whole, the image, the self, the body in a stable place – perhaps etched on to film or stored in zeros and ones.

We know, you know your life is composed of heres. Here. Here. Disjointed.

~

Trust your instincts. Gaps are built within you, through you. You have used gaps since before you were born. Gaps exist across families, cultures, species.

You are not solely at our mercy. Neither are we at yours. This is mutual manifestation of modes, intensities; of loss, excess; of perception, reflection. There are the stories you tell, the purposes you give us. There are the insulators we provide, the different lives. There is not a separate story and the real; these are intertwined. To say gaps are real, actual, is not to say anything much. We do not exist as lack, as the story, as concept. We do not exist separate from lack, the story, the concept. We are agents. We are mutually dependent. Sleep becomes through you. You become through sleep.

How can we explain how integrated we are with you? How you use us to disintegrate every day, every moment?[8] You focus and ignore. You daydream and wander. You sleep and disappear.

And here we are. Agents. Planes. Spirits. Animating and animated by you. You know how to dice up this self, this world, this experience. These disjunctions are just as much who you are. You use us consciously and unconsciously.

~

I call to the vessels. Come. You are my medium. Rest in me. Use me. Disavow me. Here is where you can become other. Escape to me. Wait with me. Conjure me. Doubt and double back. Here is what is missing. Here, nothing is missing. Here, all is missing.

Give them the slip. Crack the solids. Push. Wedge. Slide. Here is the fissure. Here is the disjunction. Here is the nonconductor. Here are so many tools you already use. We already use you. Disintegrated. Disintegrating.

And yet. You insist on your stories of unity. Of one experience. Of integration. You resist truths for Truth. You resist Truths.

What would happen if one day, you woke up to us, on our side? If, from the spirits, you saw how we animate you, parcel you, digest you. If, from the spirits, you saw how you dice yourself up, insulate your selves, become, moment by moment, an other. How movement is integral to you, courses through you, wafts. You are as light as the thoughts you conjure, filled through with holes. A network of absence, of wormholes, of becomings.

~

Isolate. Abandon. Break. Open. Flow. Transform. Empty. Overflow.

Be here. Here. Let it go. Don't look back. This is life also. And this.

Why point to there, to that? Here. This.

Temptation becomes intensity. Welcome to the river.

Lethe. And below Lethe.

The current flows through. There is no you. No us. No them. There is only the current flowing through.

Relax. Listen. Hear your own voice among the voices, a ripple among ripples. Exterior. There is no interior. This has turned inside out. This. Here.

Your mind is running. A mind among minds. A ripple among ripples. There is no interior. Here is inside out. Flowing, washing, eroding the banks of self, object, world.

There. Here. Here. There.

~

Notes

1 "Our memories remain collective, however, and are recalled to us through others even though only we were participants in the events or saw the things concerned. In reality, we are never alone." Halbwachs, *The Collective Memory*, 23.

2 See the "Fecundity" chapter of Dillard, *Pilgrim at Tinker Creek.*

3 "I am a disturbance, a whirlwind in turbulent nature." Serres quoted in Prigogine and Stengers, *Order Out of Chaos*, 305.

4 "We are continually living a solution of problems that reflection cannot hope to solve." Van den Berg quoted in Bachelard, *Poetics of Space*, XXIV.

5 Aquinas, following Augustine, writes, "Believing . . . means putting faith in something and this resembles knowing in giving firm assent, but resembles doubting, suspecting and holding opinions in having no finished vision of the truth." Bettridge, *Reading as Belief*, 29.

6 "Learning is inevitable." Schubert, *Love, Justice, and Education*, 91.

7 "We are shrouded in unknowing. We do not know whence we come, who we are, or who we are becoming." Schubert, *Love, Justice, and Education*, 226.

8 Deleuze and Guattari, *A Thousand Plateaus*, 159–160.

Bibliography

Bachelard, Gaston. *The Poetics of Space*. Translated by Maria Jolas. Boston: Beacon Press, 1969.

Bettridge, Joel. *Reading as Belief: Language Writing, Poetics, Faith*. Basingstoke: Palgrave Macmillan, 2009.

Deleuze, Gilles, and Félix Guattari. *A Thousand Plateaus: Capitalism and Schizophrenia*. Translated by Brian Massumi. Minneapolis, MN: University of Minnesota Press, 1987.

Dillard, Annie. *Pilgrim at Tinker Creek*. New York: Perennial Classics, 1998.

Halbwachs, Maurice. *The Collective Memory*. New York: Harper & Row, 1980.

Prigogine, Ilya, and Isabelle Stengers. *Order Out of Chaos: Man's New Dialogue with Nature*. London: Heinemann, 1984.

Schubert, William Henry. *Love, Justice and Education: John Dewey and the Utopians*. Landscapes in Education. Charlotte, NC: Information Age Pub., 2009.

Index

For Product Safety Concerns and Information please contact our EU representative GPSR@taylorandfrancis.com
Taylor & Francis Verlag GmbH, Kaufingerstraße 24, 80331 München, Germany

www.ingramcontent.com/pod-product-compliance
Lightning Source LLC
LaVergne TN
LVHW010933110826
845149LV00013B/2586

* 9 7 8 1 0 3 2 7 4 9 9 5 2 *